BEING LETTERS FROM WESTERN CANADA 1911-13

The land of open doors

J. BURGON BICKERSTETH

WITH A NEW INTRODUCTION BY THE AUTHOR

UNIVERSITY OF TORONTO PRESS
Toronto and Buffalo

Toronto and Buffalo
Reprinted in paperback 2014
ISBN 978-0-8020-2181-6 (cloth)
ISBN 978-0-8020-6266-6 (paper)
LC 76-41611
CN ISSN 0085-6207

Social History of Canada 29

This book has been published with the help of a grant from the Canada Council.
The Land of Open Doors: Being Letters from Western Canada was originally published in London in 1914 by Wells Gardner, Darton & Co. Ltd.

An introduction

BY J. BURGON BICKERSTETH

IT HAS BEEN DECIDED to republish *The Land of Open Doors*, which has long been out of print, in the hope that it may be of use to those who are taking an increasing interest in the pioneer days of the West particularly during the early years of this century. In contributing this new introduction to my letters written over sixty years ago, I will try to recall very briefly the events which lay behind the formation of the Archbishops' Western Canada Mission and how it happened that I personally became involved in what proved to be a fascinating experience and one of high adventure.

It is common knowledge that from 1901 to 1914 (and even in a modified degree until 1916) the population of that vast territory lying between the eastern boundary of Manitoba and the mountains increased on an unprecedented scale. Year by year settlers in their tens of thousands poured into what became known after 1905 as the three prairie provinces when the provinces of Saskatchewan and Alberta were created, Manitoba having become a province in 1870. The settlers came from the United Kingdom, from the United States, from every part of Canada, and from Europe, intent on acquiring land offered by the federal government on extremely reasonable terms. Moreover, these same years saw a vast network of new railroads spreading through the West and by 1910 two transcontinental lines, the Grand Trunk Pacific and the Canadian Northern, were converging on the Yellowhead Pass almost side by side and were faced with a long and arduous building program over the Great Divide into British Columbia. The demand for unskilled labour, which had existed for many years, now became formidable indeed and trainloads of foreign-speaking manual workers of many nationalities but mostly from southern Europe flooded into Saskatchewan and Alberta.

This vast migration was nothing less than Canada's 'Great Trek,' the like of which she will probably never see again, and if it created administrative difficulties for the federal government and also for the three provincial governments, it likewise presented problems of great complexity to the various religious communions already operating in these western regions. For some years the Anglican Church had been making gallant efforts to meet this critical situation from her own resources, but by 1909 it became clear that this was no longer possible and it was then that Dr. Matheson, the Archbishop of Rupert's Land, wrote to Randall Davidson, the

Archbishop of Canterbury, appealing for help from the church of the old country. Davidson with characteristic caution sent out one of his chaplains, the Reverend W.G. Boyd, to western Canada to size up the whole situation and report how help could best be given. This was in the fall of 1909 and the result of Boyd's visit was a joint letter signed by the Archbishop of Canterbury and by Cosmo Lang, the Archbishop of York, which appeared in *The Times* and other leading newspapers on 26 February 1910. It was addressed significantly enough not only to the Church of England but also to the people of England. This was a most unusual course for the two archbishops to take and it attracted widespread attention.

The archbishops appealed for four things in logical order – for interest and prayer, and for men and money – and they asked the mother church to send out to the young hard-pressed church in the West fifty men (clergy and laymen) each year for the next ten years. From the first it was agreed with the Canadian bishops that the help which the mother church now offered should be limited to ten years in the expectation that by 1920 the church in Saskatchewan and Alberta would be able to stand on its own feet. Clergy were asked to offer their services for four years or longer and laymen for two years or longer, each man, whether priest or layman, to receive £2 a month as pocket money with the cost of board, lodging, and travelling paid by the Mission. Furthermore, the Canadian bishops asked the Archbishops' Mission to concentrate on three areas which they felt most needed help. In each of these areas there would be a separate branch of the Mission with its own headquarters in Edmonton, Cardston, and Regina. The priests (each with a layman if possible) were to move out over the territory allotted to their respective Mission forming new districts which eventually would become parishes; they themselves were to live among the new settlers at some strategic point, only returning to the headquarters of their particular Mission from time to time for consultation and refreshment, bodily and spiritual.

The response to the joint letter was immediate. Within a few weeks the first group of clergy, having been vetted for the work in hand, were accepted, and Boyd, who had been appointed head of the Edmonton Mission, arrived in Edmonton on 1 May 1910 accompanied by three priests and three laymen. They were followed by the Reverend Douglas Ellison, who arrived in Regina in August 1910 to form the headquarters of the Railway Mission – so-called because the outlying settlements it planned to serve could be reached by the railways then rapidly being built in the southern part of Saskatchewan. Finally, well before the end of 1910, Canon W.H. Mowat had established the headquarters of the Southern Alberta Mission at Cardston in the centre of the Mormon belt. It can thus be seen that the original appeal of Archbishop Matheson received a speedy and enthusiastic response from the old country.

How was it that in 1910 a young man of twenty-two years of age and in his final year at Oxford became involved in this exciting adventure? I could claim no special knowledge of Canada and had no friends there except a few Canadian Rhodes scholars whom I had met at Oxford and whom I liked and admired. Certainly it had never entered my head to visit Canada, still less to take up work there.

It happened in this way. One evening early in April 1910 I was sitting in my rooms in Christ Church, Oxford, hard at work as my final examinations were uncomfortably near. There was a knock on the door and in came W.G. Boyd. I did not know him at all well and so wondered why he had called on me. The object of his visit soon became clear. Would I consider joining the Archbishops' Western Canada Mission when I had taken my degree? I at least knew roughly to what he was referring because, like many others, I had read the joint letter of the two archbishops when it appeared in *The Times* the previous February. Astonished at this suggestion I replied that, although my family had for many generations served the church in different parts of the world, I myself had no intention whatever of being ordained and in any case had never thought of going to Canada. Boyd pointed out that from the first it had been planned that laymen were to play an important part in the activities of the Western Canada Mission and it was hoped that those who offered themselves for this work would come from different types of background and possess different gifts and different skills, any or all of which would prove valuable in enabling them to assist the clergy. He told me that he had recently returned from a lengthy visit to the West, where he had made a careful study of the whole situation, and was shortly returning to Alberta to take charge of the Edmonton Mission. He hoped I might be interested in joining it as a layman for two years and seeing for myself the wonderful things which were happening at that very moment in western Canada.

Naturally I asked for time to consider this startling proposal, which I at once saw might well affect the whole course of my life. I had a further talk with Boyd before he returned to Edmonton and I then told him that after consultation with my parents and others, all of whom were well qualified to give me sound advice, I was prepared to have a shot at it, although I considered myself singularly unfitted to help the clergy or for that matter any of the people then pouring into the West. It was decided that I should stay up at Oxford for a few months and do some reading with a view to my new work and then in May 1911 join the Mission for two years – long enough, Boyd assured me, to familiarize myself with the new settlers and their problems. He added that one of my special jobs besides the Mission work would be to keep in touch with the young University of Alberta because in due course it might be possible to establish an ordinary residential (not a theological) college in what would, without doubt, become one of the leading academic institutions in Canada. I must admit that this idea, vague and unformulated as it necessarily was at this early state (although even then welcomed by the university authorities) was an added incentive to the decision I had already taken to try my luck in the West. It struck a spark.

After rereading these letters I think I can say that they succeed in giving a reasonably vivid and accurate account of life in western Canada as I saw it over sixty years ago in the raw. If some of the judgements I make seem dogmatic and severe and others immature and superficial it must be borne in mind that they were essentially *personal* letters written with no idea of publication to his parents by a young man in his early twenties who was completely captivated by Canada and thrilled by the amazing events he was witnessing day by day in the West. When Lord Grey, who had recently been Governor General of Canada, saw one of the earlier letters he asked to see others as they became available, but wisely added that I must on no account be told this, and it was not long before he told my mother that he thought the letters should eventually be published although this also should be unknown to me. In the event it was not till July 1913 when I returned to England and had been able to talk with my parents and later with Lord Grey that I learnt about this plan and was urged by him not to alter a single word in the letters except to see that they contained no glaring errors of fact and that the punctuation was correct. I followed this advice but thought it proper to give fictitious names to the people I had met although it turned out that this was quite unnecessary as they quickly recognized who everybody was and the fact that they were mentioned at all gave them pleasure rather than offence. After all, I never made critical, still less malicious, comments about individuals for the simple reason that no one, as far as I could remember, ever provided me with the material to do so.

As I moved about my district in the first year among the homesteaders and in the second year among the railroad builders, I usually found an opportunity to scribble down the gist of a conversation or the main facts of some striking episode shortly after these occurred. For instance, it was my invariable practice, having spent the night in a camp (it might be on the grade miles beyond the end of steel), to sit down on a log next morning at a discreet distance from the camp and before proceeding on my way to jot down the actual words of the racy back-chat of the camp cook or the details of my encounter with a group of tough, blasphemous but large-hearted men in a filthy hut the night before. Thus these letters were written hot and reflected my actual impressions at the moment. They are now republished intact and the modern reader will find much which will strike him as odd, not least perhaps the slang words and phrases which I found it was necessary to explain in a footnote for the benefit of readers in the old country unfamiliar with Canada and the United States. The title of the book itself may seem somewhat precious although it was chosen not so much to suggest the countless opportunities which in a new country undoubtedly awaited the hard-working and imaginative settler as to emphasize the sheer kindness and hospitality of the good-hearted people who became my real friends.

In June 1913 my time with the Mission ended. I was preparing to return to England but was offered by the president and accepted a lectureship in the University of Alberta. After the kind of life I had been living, a period of serious study was obviously essential. In the event I was accepted as a graduate student at the Sorbonne and from September 1913 to June 1914 spent a fascinating year in Paris. A few days before I was due to return to Canada the war broke out. I enlisted in the British Army as a private in August 1914 and then served as an officer in the Royal Dragoons until 1919, seeing much active service in France.

Demobilized in May 1919, I returned to Canada in August to take up my long delayed lectureship. Although welcomed by an outstanding professorial staff and from the first fascinated by my close contact with the undergraduates, I nonetheless realized by the end of my second year that I was in no way fitted for a career which perforce entailed so much direct teaching. Most reluctantly, therefore, I resigned. On my way back to England I was offered, while in Toronto, the wardenship of Hart House – a post of immense possibilities but involving no teaching. After some hesitation I accepted it. I thus passed through another 'open door' to what was to prove for better or for worse my life work.

The land of open doors

TO

MY FATHER

STEEL ENTERING TÊTE JAUNE CACHE, JULY 1912 (*see page* 215)

FOREWORD

NEARLY fifty years ago a young Presbyterian minister, James Robertson, born 1839, swore that, God helping him, he would never allow the Canadian Prairie to become a "wild and woolly West." He refused a good call from New York, preferring to serve his own country at a quarter of the salary within his reach. He felt that his own people wanted him, and, as he expressed it, "the time for self is gone." Before 1870 the great West was regarded with fear as the great lone land of terrible Arctic winters, and as an extremely doubtful asset to the Dominion. James Robertson heard the tread of the coming millions. Facing blizzards and the frosts of winter, he showed the path to service, which has been admirably trod by the writer of these letters. His motto was: "We must live in the future here."

When I was in Canada I was so much impressed by the influence of the character and work of James Robertson on the moulding of Western developments, that I suggested to the people of Winnipeg that they could not choose a better subject for the first statue to be erected in their city.

More than fifty years ago a young Roman Catholic of French-Canadian descent, Father Lacombe, twelve years older than Robertson, devoted himself with equal energy and disinterestedness to missionary effort in the same field. At that time the Church of England, which appeared to be more concerned with teaching men how to believe than how to act, was not conspicuous, as were the Presbyterian and Roman Catholic Churches, for its missionary zeal either among the Indians or the pioneers of Western Canada. But the dogmatic entrenchments which formerly filled the greater part of the picture of the Church of England in Canada, to the comparative exclusion of other subjects, have been pushed into the background. A new virility is stirring her limbs; and just as we bared our heads before the work of James Robertson the Presbyterian minister, and of the Roman Catholic Father, Albert Lacombe, so now we may feel just pride in contemplating the disinterested devotion of the young clergy of the Church of England, who are daily rendering services the performance of which frequently requires a moral courage of a higher order than that which has so often secured the Victoria Cross.

In January 1913 I was staying in a house in Glasgow with a fellow guest, who had in her possession a letter just received from Mr. J. B. Bickersteth, a lay missionary who, with other members of the Archbishops' Mission, was endeavouring, with the courage and disinterestedness of a soldier leading a forlorn hope, to meet so far as possible the spiritual requirements of the settlers and the men engaged in construction work of the Grand Trunk Pacific Railway. The perusal of this letter left a deep impression upon my mind. It had been written under conditions which would have prevented most men from writing at all, and was remarkable not only for its contents, which had flowed naturally and unreservedly from the pen of a son writing in fullest confidence to his parents, but for the artistic excellence inherent in a singularly clear and beautiful handwriting, as well as for the marks of culture, accurate observation, and humour which were apparent in every sentence. Nor did the distinction of the handwriting excel the interest of its contents. They revealed with the vividness of a cinematograph the privations, sufferings, tragedies, and comedies inseparable from the lives of those whose adventurous spirit has led them to undertake the initial spadework upon the foundations of a future civilisation which, it is hoped, will some day make Western Canada renowned for noble living and for high ideals.

I was so impressed and fascinated by the letter that I begged to be included in the list of those who might share the pleasure of reading future letters from the same pen. That privilege was granted to me, and I can honestly say that few pleasures enjoyed during the year 1913 exceeded that of reading these letters as they arrived.

They will speak for themselves. They describe the scenes witnessed by the writer, and the impressions left upon his mind. They are the letters of a man in whom accuracy of observation, sympathy, sense of proportion, poise, courage, humour, self-forgetfulness, and whole-hearted devotion to the service of God and man are all conspicuous.

I hope they may be widely read; and that they may create in the hearts of many of those who eat bread baked from the wheat of the Canadian West, and of those whose wealth has been made possible by the work of the men described therein, a sense of moral responsibility for the conditions in which those men labour and live; conditions which all lovers of the Church, the Empire, and Humanity should desire to make brighter and more attractive. To those who share this desire the opportunity of giving practical effect to it is before them.

GREY.

INTRODUCTION

"The Nineteenth Century was the Century of the United States, the Twentieth Century belongs to Canada." Some such dictum is said to have originated with Sir Wilfred Laurier while he was Premier. "I do not deny that in a period of rapid development, such as that which has characterised the progress of Canada, you will perhaps find the spirit of the market-place showing a keener development than it might at some other periods of a nation's history." So spoke Mr. Borden, as Premier of the Dominion, on his memorable visit to London in the summer of 1912.

No one who has lived in the West for any length of time would be prepared to deny the truth of either of these statements. Canada even yet is on the threshold of her great development, and to a large extent her people is obsessed with the spirit of the market-place. Money-making mania! It is not to be wondered at. Given untold resources, and therefore endless opportunities for accumulating wealth, how could it be otherwise? But therein lies the danger. A nation cannot live by bread alone.

Mr. Michael Sadler describes the successful man from the North American Continent as one "who, characterised by a new and venturesome optimism, is self-confident, insatiable in his appetite for new experiences and sensations, buoyant, swift-minded, gay, but often ruthless towards the incompetent, quick but fickle in his intimacies, humorously tolerant in his judgments, stoical in danger, unfrightened of the future, though uncertain of the issue the future may bring." Add to this an untiring devotion to the *pursuit* of money (not so much devotion to money itself), and the picture is complete. It is a true representation of the kind of man bred by the West.

Into a country which produces this type of character, and into an atmosphere permeated with the ideas of the market-place, has been pouring for the last ten years a vast horde of people of every nationality. They come from Eastern America, from the middle West and from the Western States; from Quebec and Ontario and the Maritime Provinces. In the British Isles there is hardly a village which has not paid its toll to Canada—hardly a family which has not some tie, direct or indirect, with the great Dominion.

Long ago the fever spread to other European countries. In 1912 over eighty thousand non-English speaking people were admitted to Canada. When the United States of America was receiving this number of foreigners, she had a population of thirty millions to absorb them, whereas the population of Canada (1913) is, roughly, between seven and eight millions—not much more than that of London and its suburbs. A large proportion of this foreign invasion finds its way quickly to the construction camps or to work of some kind on the railway. Such are the Galicians, Italians, and other Southern Europeans. The Germans, Scandinavians, and Northern Europeans are generally to be found on the land. They have been attracted by the magic of property, and are usually more permanent settlers than the Southerners, whose numbers are likely to fall off when the great demand for labour on the railroad becomes less insistent. But it will be many years before there is no demand for this kind of labour, and as long as foreigners can return to their native country better endowed with this world's goods than when they left it, others will continue to follow their example and try their fortune in the new land.

The returned emigrant is the finest publicity agent there is. A visit from the successful settler to his native village makes a deeper impression on the bucolic mind than scores of pamphlets. And only the shipping agents have any idea of the many hundreds of people, English-speaking and foreign, who year by year return to their native country in Europe to visit friends for a while, or comfortably to end their days there.

Not only many nationalities but countless types of religious belief are represented by the new citizens of Canada. According to the last census (1911) the different creeds to be found in the Dominion, with its population of little more than seven millions, number seventy-nine.[1] True, some of these religious sects cannot boast a large membership. For instance, there are 14 "Exclusive Brethren," 42 "Marshallites," 407 "Millennial Dawnites," and 28 "Apostles." "Daniel's Band" numbers 64. The "Saints of God" account for 39; the "Saints" for 297.

Over 6,000,000 of the people are either Anglicans (1,043,017), Methodists (1,079,892), Presbyterians (1,115,324), or Roman Catholics (2,833,041). Of the Roman Catholic membership, 2,000,000 are French Canadian. The interesting point is this. Comparing these figures of 1911 with those of 1901, the Anglican percentage of increase, during the ten years, is 53.03 per cent.—far greater than the increase of any of the other denominations. This is due, no doubt, to the large influx of English people; and if the same proportion of increase among all these four religious bodies continues, the Anglican Church will before long surpass numerically the Methodists and Presbyterians, as she already does the English-speaking Roman Catholics.

And so year after year this great army of settlers, with its curious assortment of languages

[1] *Cf.* p. 265 for the extraordinary list of different religious bodies to be found in Canada to-day.

and creeds, presses into Canada. Many of these home-seekers are coming to new climatic conditions—all (except perhaps the Americans) are going into an atmosphere of new ideas. As the spirit of the country gets hold of them, a severance of old traditions and a re-setting of ideals is inevitable. Old interests change; principles, once firm, become lax; the entire outlook seems different; the whole life is transplanted. Sometimes a man's religion is not sufficiently hardy to flourish, or even to *live*, in the severer climate of the new land.

What is the motive at the bottom of this great movement? What is it which causes men and women to root up old associations, to leave old friends, and set out for a distant land? Undoubtedly it is the wish to avail themselves of the opportunities which a new country alone can offer for attaining success in every department of life. We came to "give the children a chance," "to possess our own land," "to better ourselves a bit," "to have more freedom." These are the kind of answers to the question "Why did you come?" And, indeed, if material prosperity is the one object in life, people are fully justified in turning their faces towards Canada with confidence. As regards her capability of producing countless acres of "No. 1 Hard," or of yielding quick returns for steady labour or fortunate speculation, intending settlers have little cause for anxiety. It is a country where human brain and human muscle are taming the forces of nature with such incredible rapidity that, provided a man is ready to work hard and intelligently, there can be little doubt of ultimate success.

But are business openings, the standard of wages, the fertility of the soil, the only questions which should exercise the mind of intending settlers? Take, for instance, the case of a married man who takes up land far away "up country." It will be admitted that for a family with young children a school is necessary. Can it be denied that a place of worship is equally essential? Many of those who come out to farm in the North-West have little idea that they may be planted down in a district miles from the nearest school and out of touch with even the farthest rounds of the travelling missionary. Many have told me what complete disillusionment was theirs on this point. To be cut off from Church, school, social intercourse of every kind—benefits which in more civilised countries were so common as hardly to be valued—comes as a rude surprise to many.

These letters aim at giving some account of the attempt which is being made by the Church to reach the settlers in that part of Alberta which lies directly north and west of Edmonton, the capital city. This tract of country is bounded on the south by the Saskatchewan River, and reaches west 250 miles to the summit of the

Yellowhead Pass in the Rocky Mountains, and north 100 miles to the Athabasca River. It is a great rolling country, well watered, and in parts heavily timbered, extremely fertile when once cleared, and rapidly filling up with settlers.

The attractive and sometimes misleading emigration booklets scattered broadcast through Europe have had in the past little to say about this part of Alberta. They invariably contain photographs of huge wheatfields which the reader is told are six miles long, or of a traction engine pulling large ploughs over limitless prairie, the farmer sitting comfortably by in his automobile.

But this is far from being a true picture of life as it is lived by the present-day homesteader in the far North-West. For the settler who has little capital, the first few years on the homestead are years of continual struggle. Receipts are few—expenses many. There are at present few railways, and therefore no real market for produce. The trails are atrocious, and make all transportation extremely difficult, and in summer sometimes practically impossible. It is to this hard-working but generous-hearted and hospitable people, whose very conditions of life tend to make them over-anxious about the things of the world, that the Church comes with her practical message of hope and encouragement, and her reminder of higher ideals than mere material success.

The tract of country above mentioned having been handed over to the northern branch of the Archbishops' Western Canada Fund, the headquarters of the new Mission were established at Edmonton in the spring of 1910. Since that date some ten or eleven country Missions have been built up at various points throughout this large territory. Each country Mission Station is itself the centre of an extensive district, and is in charge of a priest, who in most cases is helped by a layman. Once in three months all the members of the Mission meet for a few days in Edmonton. Letter VII gives an account of one of these Reunions.

After a few days at headquarters, I was sent out to Lac la Nonne, one of the country Missions about sixty miles north-west of Edmonton. The Rev. G. D. Whitaker had already been in charge of this district for some little time, and during the next twelve months we did our best to work a district 100 miles long and about 20 miles broad. I was made responsible for the north-western part of this newly settled country. It took me about two weeks to make the round of my district, travelling in summer on horseback, in winter in a sleigh. Letters IV and V give some account of the earlier of these journeys.

A year later Greencourt, which is the most central settlement of this north-western district, was made the headquarters of a separate country

Mission, and was put in charge of the Rev. W. R. Ball. Interest in the work of the Mission gradually increased, and finally the people decided to build a place of worship. In June 1913 the opening services were held in the new lumber church. Western architecture is not elaborate. Building materials are expensive, and the people are not rich. But if they cannot help by making a large monetary contribution, they can and do give (what is equally valuable) their time. The history of Greencourt is similar to that of many of the other country districts, and is typical of the work which the Edmonton Mission is trying to do throughout the territory entrusted to it.

In June 1912, I was sent out due west along the line of the Grand Trunk Pacific Railway Company. My headquarters were at a camp about 140 miles west of Edmonton, where at that time a large number of men were engaged in constructing some cement works. This camp has now become a permanent settlement, and a church has been built, the material and labour being given almost entirely by the men themselves. Every month I made two trips farther west, often not going beyond the summit of the Yellowhead Pass (the limit of the diocese), but occasionally travelling many miles into British Columbia beyond the end ot steel. Letters VIII, IX, X, and XI deal with my life at Marlboro, the name subsequently given to the Cement Works, and with my experiences in the lumber and railway construction camps. Letter XII was written after a visit to the Rev. Oswin Creighton, who at the Bishop's request left the Mission to take over a large district in Central Alberta.

The aim of this book, then, is to give a straightforward account of our everyday life in North-Western Canada—a life of some discomfort, of occasional hardship, but most certainly of absorbing interest and unique opportunity. In order to present as vivid a picture as possible, I was advised to keep the account of my experiences in the original form in which they were given, namely, the letters which I sent home during the course of two years' work as a layman on the Edmonton Mission. Such letters, written at odd times and often under difficult conditions, can hardly be distinguished by literary merit. But defects in style may possibly be excused by the reader, if he feels that the book leaves on his mind some impression of the marvellous things which are going forward in the Far West to-day, and of the great efforts which the Church is making to cope with a situation unparalleled in the history of the world.

> "I pray you, in your letters, . . .
> Speak of me as I am; nothing extenuate,
> Nor set down aught in malice."
>
> *Othello*, Act v. sc. 2.

Introduction

To the Grand Trunk Pacific Railway, who have always shown us much courtesy, to the Colonial and Continental Church Society, and to Mr. Vincent Hope (engineer, Canadian Northern Railway) I am greatly indebted for permission to publish several photographs; also to the Editor of *Church Life* (Toronto) and to the Rev. W. G. Boyd, Head of the Edmonton Mission, for allowing me to make free use of an article on the need for country hospitals. Further, I am extremely grateful to Mr. Boyd for several valuable suggestions and corrections. No one but myself is responsible for any inaccuracies which may remain in the following pages, nor do the opinions therein expressed necessarily represent those of other members of the Mission.

CONTENTS

THE LAND OF OPEN DOORS

IN MID-ATLANTIC

C.P.R. ATLANTIC SERVICE, s.s. *Lake Champlain.* BETWEEN QUEBEC AND MONTREAL, *May 10th.*

WE have had a successful voyage, though a slow one, to-day being our twelfth day out from Liverpool. In mid-Atlantic the weather was rough, and on one occasion we only made 198 knots in twenty-four hours. 1450 people, all told, on board: 1080 steerage passengers—the rest second-class. It has been extremely interesting seeing something of the kind of people who are pouring into Canada by their thousands. Dallas[1] has been acting as Chaplain, and we have spent most of our time in the steerage, getting to know the people. They are a curious mixture. There are a great many Irish, mostly from Belfast—some are Roman Catholic and some Protestant. The bitterness that exists between them is incredible. A Protestant child gets extra sugar in its tea when it learns to say "Damn the Pope," and a

[1] The Rev. W. L. S. Dallas, like myself on the way to join the Edmonton Mission, and while in Canada supported by the Parish of St. Mary Abbots, Kensington.

Roman Catholic is taught to regard the Protestant with equal detestation. This party spirit they have not left behind. The other night there was a steerage concert got up by the Protestants. The Roman Catholics ran a rival show at the other end of the ship.

We have held many services, and have always been well received. The first Sunday evening we had service in the steerage saloon, which was simply packed. The place was rather greasy and smelly; the rough wooden tables and benches, the companion ladders and passages, and every inch of floor space were crammed with men, women, and children. A service with plenty of singing breaks the monotony of the voyage, and, if for no other cause, is welcomed by the people. Time hangs heavily on their hands. But for other reasons too it was undoubtedly appreciated. After all, everyone there had said good-bye to many of those they loved, and had closed a big chapter in their life; and when one is steaming towards a great strange land, where everything will be new and unfamiliar, hearts are naturally open to deep emotions.

Here are a few types I have got to know better than others:—

1. Husband, with wife and nine children, the latter all under twelve years of age. In England he had never earned more than 18*s.* a week. Out of it he had saved enough money to emi-

grate with the help of the Church Army; hoping to farm eventually.

2. Young Englishman from Cornwall, going out to get work in salmon business at New Westminster, British Columbia.

3. Englishman, very Westernised, going back, after a holiday, to his ranch east of Edmonton.

4. Man, with wife and three children, from Watford, going to Sudbury, Ontario, to work in railway shops for the C.P.R.

5. An Italian, been for a holiday in Italy, and now returning to railway job in West.

6. Seedy-looking clerk—going to some office appointment in Vancouver.

7. An old man of sixty, farmed in Australia and knocked about everywhere, going to buy land in Alberta.

8. A substantial farmer from near Basingstoke, with wife and children, hoping to fruit-farm in British Columbia; he and his ancestors had been tenants on same estate for over 200 years. Why emigrate, then? "Farmer's job no good nowadays, and I want to do the best for my children," was his answer.

9. Elderly man, long earned £72 a year in Stock Exchange office—not good enough—so off to try his luck in Canada.

10. Chemist's assistant, saved a little capital, hoping to start on his own in the West.

And so on; I could give you a list pages long.

The Land of Open Doors

Two days ago we sighted Cape Gaspé, in the province of Quebec—a wild, desolate-looking country, with hills still covered with snow, deep ravines, and little fishing villages clustering in sheltered spots. We coasted along the southern shore of the St. Lawrence—still so broad that one could not grasp it was a river. Yesterday, however, the northern shore came into view, and the river narrowed to an appreciable size. To sail up the St. Lawrence is certainly the fitting way to approach Canada for the first time. It is an amazing river. The hills rise steeply on either side, with higher ranges behind; villages and small townships straggle along the shore in an almost continuous line. Gradually the hills recede, and give place to sloping pasture land and small farms.

About 5 P.M. we stopped for medical inspection, which is held merely to see there is no infectious disease on board. Later there is another stricter inspection. We all go before three or four officials, one of whom is a doctor. "Where are we going? What are we going to do? Have we each got twenty-five dollars?" It is all entered on a large form, and we receive in return an inspection card with a medical and civil examination stamp, and are told to keep it carefully for three years. If the doctor sees anything suspicious he can, and often does, forbid entry into the country. The Captain told me he had seen heartbreaking scenes on the quay at Quebec—wives separated from husbands and children from parents—sent back in the same ship by ruthless immigration officials.

Last night everyone was on deck eagerly awaiting the first sight of Quebec. It was a glorious evening, with a golden haze in the west —a few stars shining, the water glassy, and the wooded banks almost black in the dusk. The ship glided silently up the river. On the for'ard deck were hundreds of steerage passengers. Somebody started a plaintive Irish air, and the crowd took it up, singing in harmony. Suddenly as we rounded a bend of the river, the twinkling lights of Quebec came into full sight—the citadel, the terrace, and the straggling town all clearly outlined by the lamps. As we drew nearer, and finally moored alongside the quay, the new citizens of Canada cheered again and again ; and, on the bridge, the Captain proudly smiled at bringing his passengers into port in such good spirits. Including our number, over 3000 immigrants had arrived at Quebec that *day*, the large majority of them bound for the West. A week hence they will be scattered all over the huge Dominion, and many illusions will have been dispersed.

The steerage passengers all landed early this morning at Quebec, and we are now steaming further up the river to Montreal, where I shall mail this.

WESTWARDS FROM MONTREAL

THE MISSION HOUSE,
EDMONTON, *May* 18*th*.

DALLAS and I arrived here two days ago. It is practically three weeks since we left Liverpool.

At Montreal we stayed three days as the guests of our kind friend Mr. Lachlan Gibb. There is nothing much to tell you about Montreal. It is like any other large well-built city, with its huge banks, churches, and business houses, and stretches from the St. Lawrence up to the lower slope of Mount Royal. For so large a place the roads, except in the centre of the city, seemed bad, and the forest of telegraph poles in the streets was ugly. We saw something of the great McGill University, which has received such rich grants from Scotch Canadians.

On Friday night we boarded the Imperial Limited Canadian Pacific Railway (C.P.R.) express, and steamed out of the station to the minute. Mr. Gibb had provided us with a hamper of eatables. Each day we cooked our own breakfast and lunch in the kitchen supplied on the train by the Company, and had dinner in the dining car. To have every meal in the dining car would have been far too expensive.

Westwards from Montreal

We passed Ottawa in the night, and all Saturday, and till late on Sunday, travelled through desolate, rocky country, studded with numerous lakes and covered with scrubby timber, uninhabited and, I should think, largely uninhabitable. The building of a railway through this country was a gigantic feat. The C.P.R. is truly marvellous—the three little letters are everywhere in evidence, and almost get on one's nerves. They seem to be on every train, hotel, steamer, and official that I have so far seen. They are stamped on the table silver and writing-paper, and worked into the blankets and sheets—even the door-mat is not exempt.

Seventy miles east of Winnipeg, the rocky waste is left behind, and the prairie comes with a rush. We reached Winnipeg Sunday evening, and walked down Main Street and Portage Avenue for an hour. Large asphalted thoroughfares, numerous street cars, several skyscrapers, huge business blocks, scores of real estate offices, hotels with men sitting in the windows, and crowds of people in the streets. I had seen so many photographs of Winnipeg that the place almost seemed familiar. What we saw was not beautiful; but in all these Western places, to be impressed, one has got to make comparisons, and in this case the comparison between Fort Garry of 1870 and the Winnipeg of to-day makes one gasp.

Next morning we were well into Saskatchewan.

As we travelled hour after hour across some of the finest agricultural land in the world, and heard of rich timber and minerals farther North and West, it was difficult to realise there was once a time when it was seriously proposed to let Canada go in favour of the island of Guadaloupe.

It was amusing getting off at various stations to stretch one's legs. The little lumber station-houses are all painted red, and two notices, *i.e.* "C.P.R. Telegraphs" and "Dominion Express Company," invariably meet the eye. All the parcel work in connection with the C.P.R. is done by the latter Company. The Canadian Express Company and the Canadian Northern Express Company have a working arrangement with the two other great Canadian railways, the Grand Trunk Pacific and the Canadian Northern. There is no parcel post, such as we have, in Canada.[1]

There is always a crowd of spitting, chewing loiterers waiting for the train to come in—strong tanned men, critical and reserved. These little prairie townships are much the same—real estate office, hotel, livery barn, general store, a few shacks, and generally a church and a school. Though laid out in parallel streets and avenues, the place generally lacks all symmetry, because the shacks are scattered about at unequal intervals and are built on different corners of the lots.

[1] This is shortly to be inaugurated.

We got out at Calgary on Tuesday morning. It seemed literally humming with life: new buildings, scaffolding, hammering and noise at every corner—Winnipeg on a smaller scale—the country round, bare undulating downs, stretching westward to the Rocky Mountains. We called on the Bishop of Calgary, who gave us the warmest of welcomes. The Bishop is an old-timer, having been over forty years in the Far West. You can imagine what changes he has seen.

The journey North to Edmonton was a little dreary—180 miles, about as far as London to Leeds. It took 7½ hours, so travelling is slow. Rain came down in torrents. We passed one go-ahead-looking place—Wetaskiwin, I think; facing the station were a number of large hoardings, "Come to Wetaskiwin, railway centre, financial hub, &c., &c. The sunny city with the sunny smile."

Mr. Boyd met us at Edmonton, or rather Strathcona, and we drove across to Edmonton proper on the other side of the Saskatchewan River.[1] The Mission House is large and comfortable, but quite simple. Kitchen, dining-room, library, and Mr. Boyd's office below; above, bedrooms and dormitory, and above that a large

[1] Strathcona and Edmonton have since been incorporated, and the C.P.R. now runs across a high-level bridge into the centre of the city.

attic, where at least ten men can sleep. The Chapel given by Sir Henry Pellatt is a beautiful little building.

Edmonton is a far pleasanter city than any other I have yet seen in the West. Its situation on the Saskatchewan River gives it a wonderful opportunity of becoming a really beautiful city. All the chief banks, hotels, and stores are situated on or near Jasper Avenue, the main thoroughfare. The residential part of the city lies mostly north and west of this. But it is expanding rapidly in every direction. It is well served with electric cars, but when one sees a city so much in the early stages, one realises how much time, money, and labour go to make up a modern town.

In this kind of weather getting about is a matter of some difficulty. The streets are only asphalted in the centre of the town—elsewhere they are a sea of thick clogging mud. We clean our own boots!

To-day I have been doing a little visiting for Mr. Boyd. Among others, I called on such a nice Irish woman. Her husband works at a large packing plant in North Edmonton. They have several children. This is their third year in this country. Their first year they lived in a tent, their second year they lived in a small two-roomed shack. This year they have built themselves a fine new house with two storeys, a balcony, concrete foundations, and everything complete—

JASPER AVENUE, EDMONTON, IN THE EARLY 'NINETIES

THE SAME THOROUGHFARE TO-DAY

(Both photographs by Brown, Edmonton)

worth 1500 dollars. The house stands on a good-sized lot—they have a good kitchen garden, also a cow and a small barn. How could this have been done in the old country? It is typical of the progress made by hundreds of hard-working, energetic families in this wonderful West.[1]

This at least is clear. One is now in a country where it is no shame to work with one's hands. Manual work is not necessarily menial work. The possession of wealth may give some kind of social pre-eminence, but the absence of it certainly does not imply social inferiority. It is a case of every man playing for his own hand, and the weakest go to the wall. I should imagine that the Yorkshire Tyke's motto fits the Westerner well:

> See all, hear all, say nowt;
> Eat all, drink all, pay nowt;
> And if tha does owt for nowt,
> Do it for thisen.

This Far West is a queer place, but very interesting. Mr. Boyd's plans for me are these: I stay here only a few days, and then go north-west of here 60 miles to Lac la Nonne, where Whitaker[2] and Jim Clare are already estab-

[1] For the whole question of Emigration, *cf.* the interesting study, *Emigration from the United Kingdom to North America*, 1763–1912, by S. C. Johnson. Routledge, 1913.

[2] The Rev. G. D. Whitaker and Jim Clare (a layman) had come out from England with the original number in May 1910, and had been living at Lac la Nonne some few months before I arrived.

lished. Lac la Nonne will be my kicking-off place for still farther journeys north-west into a country which we have reason to think is well settled, but where services have never yet been held.

FIRST EXPERIENCE OF WESTERN TRAILS

LAC LA NONNE, ALBERTA
(60 miles N.W. of Edmonton),
June 8th.

LET me give you some account of our journey up here from Edmonton.

There was so much to be done that it was almost mid-day before a start was made. We had a buggy with Canterbury between the shafts, and also a horse, which we had meant to let run behind, but one of us had to ride it as the buggy was so full. You know how limited the carrying capacity of a buggy is—room for two people sitting, and a little space for a few things under the seat, and that is all. Our load consisted of two chairs, several boxes of stores, oats, saddles, ropes, and other necessaries.

We left the Mission House at 2.30 amid much laughter, and certainly we did look a cheering sight. The buggy resembled a travelling gipsy cart. Canterbury, who thoroughly looks his part, being rather a grand, staid, and handsome old chocolate horse, pulled splendidly. We started out in a north-westerly direction till we struck the main trail. After about ten miles we came to St. Albert, one of the prettiest little towns I have seen so far. It lies on the Sturgeon River. When we had crossed the wooden bridge, and gone up the other side of the hill, we looked back. In the afternoon sunlight it seemed quite picturesque, if any Western town, composed of wooden shacks and one or two hotels and stores, can look picturesque.

The country was fairly flat, and had evidently been settled up for a good many years. The soil looked rich and the farms prosperous. We struck off northwards some miles beyond St. Albert, and made for Ray. It consists of a school, one or two farms, and one "stopping place," kept by a Dutchman. We watered and fed our horses, and had supper ourselves, it being now about 6 P.M. Twenty-five cents (1*s.*) each for the horses and twenty-five cents each for us—very reasonable, I thought. There is, of course, only one eating-room in these places, and all the family sat down to tea with us.

After supper I got talking to a fellow in the barn, while I was hitching up.

"Looks pretty nice land round here," I began.

"Not too bad—worth about 30 to 35 dollars an acre." And he looked at me sharply. "New to the country?"

"Yes."

"Guess you've not been long in Canada?"

"Not many weeks," I said, feeling as if I must look very green.

"Well, young fellow, I've been in this Western country quite a time, and, believe me, the best way of setting about things is, *Do* a man as he would *do* you—only *do* him first. Guess you're looking for land up here?"

"No, going to do Missionary work."

"Oh," he said, "you're a preacher, are you?" and was silent for a moment. "There's just three fellows I've no use for," he continued at last, as he took a bite at a black plug of tobacco; "the real estate man, the lawyer, and the preacher. The first two are so crooked, guess they can't lie straight in bed."

"And what about the preacher?"

"Well, I guess I'm kind of hard on preachers. Had too much church when I was a kid."

This seems a common complaint among the men out here.

"Where was that?"

"Guess I was raised in the States," he answered.

"You used to go to church there?"

"You bet your life I did when I was a kid. Went to Sunday-school regular, and knew all about it too!"

"And you've never been since you came up here?"

"Well, there isn't much to go to round here unless you're a Catholic. Still I did go to one meeting oncet (once). A fellow came round and asked us all to go the next Sunday to a shack about a mile from where I live. We all turned up, the ladies in their best clothes; I guess they like meetings, as they get the chance of chewing the rag[1] a bit and showing off their joy rags. The preacher came a bit late, he'd had a meeting somewheres else in the morning. He was as good as a circus, that man! Talk about a flea on a griddle. Why, he was jumping around all over the place while he was preachin', and he went on close on an hour. Say, he was a good listener when he talked, that fellow, believe me!"

"It doesn't seem to have done you much good."

"Shucks! I never thought it would! I just went to please the fellow, that's all. How he lived beats me."

"Didn't the people support him?"

"He had a collection at the end of the meeting, but that didn't amount to much. I'll tell you right now—when it comes to paying the preacher, there's an awful bunch of people in this country who think their money's a burden, and it ain't fair to bind any of your burdens on other people's shoulders. There's something like that in the Bible, I guess? Still we want a few

[1] Western slang for having a good gossip.

MAIL CROSSING PEMBINA RIVER ON THE FERRY

"BOB" IN A BAD MOOD

THE HOMESTEADER'S CASTLE

preachers in here all the same. It doesn't cut any ice[1] what people *say* anyway. Just go right ahead, and do the best you can, and you'll find them all right."

We left shortly after 7 P.M., and decided to get to the other side of Rivière Qui Barre and camp in the Indian Reserve, but the horses were tired, and we did not make very good progress. At last we saw Qui Barre, a place which has been left rather in a backwater as regards railways. The Canadian Northern from Edmonton to Athabasca Landing leaves it ten miles to the west, and the main line of the same railway branches off at St. Albert, and so runs about eleven miles south. Considering Rivière Qui Barre is the centre of a good farming country, and consists of two hotels, boarding-houses, stores, creamery, church, &c., it deserves better treatment. It just proves how important railways are if a place is really to go ahead. It is a French-speaking town, the church being Roman Catholic. It is the usual half-way place for us each time we go to and from Edmonton.

We stopped only to ask whether the trail through the Indian Reserve was passable, as in wet weather the mud-holes are very bad. The hotelkeeper said the trail was fair, so we decided to go on. It was now dusk.

After entering the Reserve we passed the

[1] Common Western phrase meaning "it does not matter."

Roman Catholic Mission and the Agent's house, and then kept a sharp look-out for good water and firewood. At last, coming to a sheltered spot near the trail where dry wood abounded, we started a fire, unhitched, and watered the horses. Having fed them and fixed them up for the night, we made up the fire, and about 1 A.M. lay down to try and sleep. It was a beautiful night, with a moon and brilliant stars, and no one knows the stars, as Stevenson puts it, who has not slept *à la belle étoile*. Personally, however, I found it rather chilly, and did not sleep at all.

At 3 A.M., when it was beginning to get light, we were both glad of an excuse to get up and start the fire again. The Northern Lights had been most beautiful while it was dark, and now the sun began to make preparations to rise. We attempted to get the horses to drink, and Whitaker spent some time in trying to find a better watering place. As we were making ready to boil some tea, the sun rose. It was perfectly glorious—for half-an-hour the sky had been a most brilliant pageant of red and gold, and then at last the light came flooding over the trees and lit up the white trunks of the poplars, making our fire look silly. It was about 4.15. We had some bread and sardines and tea; the latter tasted very nasty, the solid milk refusing to melt, and staying like a piece of soap at the bottom of the jam-pot which served as a kettle.

While reading Matins, we were rather disturbed in the middle of the Psalms by Canterbury rolling on the grass a few feet from us. When he does this he makes the most unearthly grunts inside, and looks most unarchiepiscopal. It upset us completely.

About 7 o'clock we made a start. The character of the country had now completely changed —no longer settled and flat, but undulating bush, through which our trail wound. We had only gone a short distance when we had to negotiate a bad mud-hole. The trail, which is generally pretty fair, comes occasionally to places where a small creek crosses it, or to swampy ground. Then it becomes a sea of mud, with generally some inches of standing water on the top, and is called a mud-hole. The horses are very apt to flounder in these, and though there is seldom danger, as is sometimes the case in a bad muskeg, it is quite possible that the horse might strain himself if he gets badly stuck.

This particular hole proved to be one of the worst. I crossed first on horseback. Charlie didn't like it, and was covered up to his belly in black slimy mud by the time he got out the other side. Canterbury tried to follow, but when a few yards in, he stuck and refused to go farther. Whitaker used the whip, and tried to rush him through, but every flounder only sent him worse in. The mud came slipping up his legs, and was soon up to his belly and above it. The buggy was stuck up to the shafts; Canterbury soon gave up struggling and simply lay there blinking, rather like an old hen on an egg, with a satisfactory expression on his face saying, "I told you so." We unhitched him with some difficulty, and lifted the shafts of the buggy. Then Whitaker stood by with the whip, I pulled with his head rope, we both shouted, and with a great effort he freed himself and stood on firmer ground, looking the most pitiable object, with mud streaming off him. Then we tried to back the buggy. This was a dismal failure, so off everything had to come, one by one. All this time we ourselves were floundering about in the mud up to our knees.

When everything was out, we lifted the back wheels one by one to loosen them, and then with two or three heaves had the beastly thing back on dry land. But we were still the wrong side, and an hour wasted. It was useless to try and find a better place to cross, and finally we had to go back to a trail we had passed the evening before, leading off rather more eastward than we wanted.

This turned out much more satisfactory, except at one place, where we stayed, I should think, three-quarters of an hour improving and making new "corduroy."[1]

[1] *i.e.* a series of tree trunks placed side by side over swampy ground, thus enabling a wagon to cross in comparative safety.

About mid-day we came to a place, or rather a district, called Sion. The only maps we have are those issued by the land authorities, and they are covered with the regular township squares. The townships are six miles long and six miles broad. They therefore contain thirty-six square miles. Each square mile is called a section. Each section is divided up into four quarter sections. The quarter section is the one hundred and sixty acres which you have heard so much about as being given free to the land seeker, and is the usual amount of land a man holds. Sometimes a family with grown-up sons will hold as much as a section between them, but it is not usual up here. Occasionally one finds a man and his son holding a half section between them, namely half a square mile. There is also the so-called "scrip"—this is land which was granted free to old soldiers who had served in the South African war, or to Indians. It is three hundred and twenty acres. This land has now, in almost every case, passed out of the hands of the original holders. The man who buys would have to fulfil the same conditions as the ordinary homesteader, but could then of course sell.

In time, there will be regular Government roads cut through the bush along the section lines every two miles east and west, and every mile north and south. They are called road allowances, and as far as Rivière Qui Barre we had been travelling on them, but farther north-west there are only the old trails, which are the sole means of communication between one place and another. They existed before the district was properly surveyed, and they are subject to all the irregularities of the country. They go round muskegs when possible, across rivers at favourable spots, avoid hills, and therefore, like any other cross-country road, are very often almost double the distance which the crow flies.

All these districts consist of scattered houses, each standing in its own quarter section, so there is never any collection of shacks or anything that reminds one of the village in the old country sense of the word. The fact that one has arrived at some particular settlement only becomes patent when one has reached the post office, generally located in a homestead occupying some central position. Further, in summer time a shack is hidden completely from its neighbour by the thick bush which covers a large part of this country.

At Sion we had dinner at a stopping place. It was the very first loghouse I had ever entered. It consisted of two rooms, both of which were divided into two by partitions about eight feet in height. It being mid-day and the family dinner hour, we all sat down together. The old people, Eastern Canadians, gave us eggs and bacon and potatoes, bread and butter, cake and jam, and rather strong tea. They were extremely pleased to see Whitaker, who read the Bible and had a prayer with them. He naturally offered to pay as we left, but the goodwife would not hear of it. We then pushed on here.

Lac la Nonne is six miles long, and runs in a north-easterly direction. We are about two miles from the schoolhouse and close neighbours to one or two homesteads which, so to speak, form the nucleus of Lac la Nonne proper.

The house stands a little above the lake with a slope of fifty yards down to the water. The lake is almost entirely surrounded by wooded country, and there is an island this end about three-quarters of a mile long, also wooded. Ducks abound. The house is lent to us by an American who keeps a store up at Mosside, about twenty-five miles north of here. We pay taxes, and he allows us to live in the house, being glad, I believe, to have it occupied. There are three good rooms —a sitting-room, where we eat and live, a bed-room, where Whitaker, Jim Clare, and I sleep, a small kitchen, and above, an attic. There is a good stable or barn, as they call it out here, plenty of outhouses, and a lot of enclosed land where we can let the horses run. But the position of the house is everything. It is perfectly glorious—prettier lake scenery you could not have. The sunsets are magnificent; every change is faithfully reflected in the water.

Two days ago we had a wedding. A family,

some distance from here, called Bentley, was marrying a daughter to a man from Eastern Canada. The wedding took place in the school, and Whitaker took it. It was a perfect day, with brilliant sunshine. By 3 P.M. there must have been a dozen teams tied up outside the schoolhouse, and thirty or forty people inside. Finally the bride and bridegroom drove up with the bride's father and mother in a buggy, and blushingly entered. Whitaker had to explain the marriage service very carefully, not only to the couple themselves, but to the whole congregation. He gave a short address, and then, after signing the register, the happy pair scrambled into the buggy amid showers of rice, and drove off. Then everybody, either riding or driving, followed them in a long line, and on arrival at the Bentleys' house we sat round and smoked while the womenkind bustled about putting the finishing touches to a large spread of cold meats and pies. Finally we sat down, about twenty-four of us, to a huge meal. The health of the newly married couple was drunk, and the home-made wedding-cake cut amid much enthusiasm. Then when all was finished there was a call for the bachelors, who were to wash up the dirty things! Whitaker and I, of course, took our share in this delectable occupation.

These people, the Bentleys, came out here from Manchester about eight years ago. You could not mistake their Lancashire accent, though in every way except this they have become Canadianised, or rather Westernised. Bentley was a carter of coal in Manchester. Having landed in Edmonton with a wife, nine children, and £80, he started out North-West by himself, found land which suited him, returned to Edmonton, and brought out his family. For years they all lived in a small log shack. The father was forced to go out to work on survey parties, sending back money for the family, and, when old enough, the two elder sons also contributed to the family exchequer by working for wages. Now he has built himself a fine big two-storeyed house, with large dining-room, kitchen, sitting-rooms, and five bedrooms. He is farming, with his sons, some five hundred acres, and possesses a large number of stock. All this rent free, with no rates and taxes (except eight dollars school tax and about the same for local improvements, *i.e.* road-making). Compare this with a small unhealthy cottage in a back street in Manchester. This man has done much for Canada, and Canada has done much for him.

What impresses me continually is the faith of the average homesteader in the North-West. He is always talking of what the country *will* be—what a fine farm his homestead will one day become, and so on. As a matter of fact, many of these men would undoubtedly find farming dull if they bought a ready-made farm. They have said as much to me. It is the actual conquering and taming of the land which has a peculiar attraction; and I think it is quite intelligible. The seeing of acre after acre gradually reclaimed from the bush and brought under cultivation constitutes the real fascination of pioneer farming.

The Americans sometimes give their children the most extraordinary names. For instance, I came across these yesterday—four small boys. The eldest was called Gladstone, after the English statesman, the second Sylvester, after Pope Sylvester, the third Edison, after the inventor, the fourth Laurier, after the Canadian Premier. Don't you think that is an amusing quartette?

We have bought a cow for thirty dollars, which is cheap. She is small, but gives plenty of milk. We are shortly going to buy a pig, so we now have quite a farm—three horses, one mare, one two-year-old, one small colt, a cow, twenty hens, a prospective pig, a dog, and a cat.

Whitaker used to have a couple of ponies called Dan and Sam. In moments of excitement their names used sometimes to get mixed up, thus causing much scandal among the faithful!

BREAKING NEW GROUND

LAC LA NONNE,
July 19th.

WE have had the heaviest rains here they have known for years. June and July are generally the two rainy months, when the trails are at their worst, and this year we have had practically seven days' continuous downpour. The trails defy all description. I have just returned from a long trip of twelve days' continual travelling, and will try and give you some account of it. It will help you to understand my life in this country.

The country north-west of Edmonton is not prairie, such as one finds in Manitoba, Saskatchewan, and Southern Alberta. Please be clear on this point. It is for the most part covered with bush. Sometimes the timber is fairly heavy, sometimes quite light. The trees are almost all poplars,[1] with thin white trunks and shimmering leaves, interspersed with occasional birch, spruce, and tamarac. True, there are stretches of open country, but they have been cleared by

[1] The poplar of the Canadian West is generally not more than twenty to thirty feet high, and bears little resemblance to the tall thin Lombardy poplar.

human labour in the past. There is no natural prairie in the ordinary sense of the word.

The trails which wind through the bush never have a chance of drying up as they would in open country, and after really wet weather, such as we have just been having, they are little better than one long mud-hole.

I left here last Thursday week on Charlie. Charlie is my horse, grey in colour, a good goer and quiet. I had a Mexican saddle; my pack fastened behind and a slicker (oilskin coat) in front. We had difficulty from the first. At the first creek of any size we came to, the bridge was "out," that is, floating on the surface of the water. The creek was only about twenty feet broad, but deep. The bridge consisted of a number of poplar trunks stretched at right angles across two larger supporting trunks, called "stringers." Being inexperienced, I did not see that the whole thing was in a more or less floating condition, and rode on to it. Charlie immediately floundered, as the bridge began to go down. I slipped off pretty sharp, keeping hold of the bridge and of Charlie, who, partly kicking the logs and partly swimming, got across somehow, bringing me, soaked to the skin and covered with mud, with him. No harm done, and I had learnt something. Charlie and I were both tired when we reached Mosside that night, having taken over eight hours to do twenty-five miles.

Next morning I went round to consult the storekeeper about the trail. I particularly wanted to reach Peavine, about thirty-five miles distant, early in the week. What did he advise?

"Well," he said, "the bridges are out; the mail carrier has not been through for eight days. He got as far as the Little Paddle River, and could not get his wagon across or swim his horses; the mud on both sides is so deep they would have been smothered before they got the chance of swimming; you can't take your horse, if you do go, and you'll probably have to swim."

And with these words he went off a mile south to get his wagon out of a bad mud-hole, where he had been forced to leave it the night before, having unhitched his four oxen.

Not very encouraging! And yet what was I to do? I knew that at any rate some of the people up there expected me. On the other hand, if I had to swim, it would be difficult to prevent the books and other contents of my pack from being ruined. However, I decided to have a shot, and, having turned Charlie loose into the storekeeper's pasture, I started off on foot with my pack on my back. It was a glorious July day, with brilliant sun and a strong breeze. After two miles I came to my first obstacle—the Little Paddle—normally a creek about thirty feet broad, now at least one hundred yards across. At the edges it was a few feet deep only, but in mid-stream the water was coming down pretty fast. The bridge, similar to the other I described, had floated off, but had fortunately stuck among some willows on this side. I clambered on to it, chose the best-looking of several thin poplar trunks sticking up close by it, and punted the whole bridge across and myself on it. It was a large ungainly raft, but perfectly safe and dry, though I had to work hard in mid-stream or should have been carried down. Having left the bridge on the other side carefully fixed, so that anyone coming from the other direction could get across to Mosside in the same manner, I proceeded on my way—ten miles through the bush—without seeing a soul except two negro children. The trail was poor; at times there were bad sloughs (pronounced *slews*) and mud-holes, where one had to wade up to one's knees in mud and water.

About 1 P.M. I arrived at Hilton's. Mrs. Hilton is a full-blooded negress, and keeps a "stopping place"—in other words an inn, if you can call two rather tumble-down log shacks by such a name. The stopping place stood in a clearing in the bush—a neat vegetable garden sloped down to the creek, which emptied into a fair-sized lake. But the trail which led across the creek, and then along the shores of the lake for half a mile, was nowhere to be seen. The lake had risen, and the creek had overflowed its banks. It looked like swimming, if I was to get across. However, dinner first, and Mrs. Hilton, with her shiny countenance and two rows of grinning white teeth, soon called me into the little shack, which served as kitchen, dining-room, and her bedroom, "stoppers" being put in two double beds in the other shack. Dinner consisted of eggs and bacon, tea, and some stewed fruit. The summer is the egg and bacon season. One seldom eats anything else as soon as one gets away from Edmonton and the vicinity of railways. In these country districts, twenty-five cents (1*s.*) is the recognised price for a meal and twenty-five cents for a bed, and the same charge is made for putting one's horse in the barn and giving him hay.

After dinner, having looked at the extent of the water, I was ready to take Mrs. Hilton's advice, and get her son-in-law to take me round in a boat. We had to go half a mile to find the boat, and then wade up to our waists to reach it. However, it saved swimming, and by 3 P.M., having paddled over the lake and across the mouth of the creek, I was landed once more on the trail. Then I had seven miles of unpleasant travelling. The trail ran through heavy timber; it was hot and close, and the mosquitoes were intolerable, as they always are when there is no breeze.

At last I came out to a large clearing, where

stood a sawmill overlooking a beautiful lake. The proprietor was a German. His wife and children were living with him in one shack—a number of men working for him lived in another. As I pounded up to the door, covered with mud from head to foot, it was hardly to be wondered that the proprietor's wife didn't know who or what I was. But directly she found out, she seemed genuinely pleased, and went to the door.

"Rudolf," she called—"Rudolf, come in at once and see the Herr Minister."

Rudolf appeared, breathless, and not too well pleased. He was a boy of nine, bare-footed and roughly dressed, but sharp as a needle.

"He knows nothing," his mother said; "he's always asking questions, but I don't know how to answer them."

Rudolf and I talked about sawmills and lumber and carpentering for some time. But before going I produced from my pack a little picture of the Crucifixion, and asked the boy if he had heard of Christ.

"Jesus Christ!" he answered, "Jesus Christ! You bet your life I have. The men are always saying it; and I say it too." I told him the story of the Crucifixion.

"Say, what sort of lumber did they use for the cross?" he asked eagerly. "Guess they had six-inch nails to drive through His hands and feet, didn't they?"

STUCK IN THE MUD

WELL OUT OF A MUD-HOLE

A YOUNG HORSE ABOUT TO BUCK
(Lac la Nonne Mission)

A TYPICAL GERMAN SETTLER

"I expect so. Anyway I'll tell you what I want you to do. Make me a cross with pieces of old lumber by the time I come round again this time next month, then I'll tell you some more."

This thoroughly interested him. To make something! He could do that.

"And look here, Rudolf, say this every night before you go to bed"; and I wrote out and explained to him the simplest of prayers, and showed him how to kneel and put his hands.

Well, it is a beginning! And, after all, this teaching of isolated children is perhaps the most valuable part of our work in these inaccessible, uncivilised parts. It is curious how little responsibility the parents seem to think rests upon them in such a case. If there is no school for week-days, and no one to hold Sunday-school, the children simply grow up without schooling, secular or religious. In one district I go to on my rounds, there must be over twenty children of school age (that is between the years of five and sixteen) in the settlement, and yet no school has been built, merely because of the bitter quarrelling as to where it is to be put.

By law, a school can be demanded by the settlers if there are twelve children of school age. A school district is formed, three trustees elected, and they are entitled to fix the amount of the taxes and are responsible for their collection. The schoolhouse must be in the middle of the district, or as near it as possible. The Education Department makes a large grant towards the salary of the teacher and other expenses, on certain conditions, and thus encourages local initiative without pauperising the people. It is an excellent system.[1] But too often it is held up by uninterested bachelors, who do not wish to have to pay the taxes, or by some other petty disagreement. Of course both a school and a church tend to increase the value of the land, and very often this is a reason for keenness in building them.

From the sawmill I had to borrow another boat to take me over a long stretch of flooded trail, and reached that night another "stopping place" kept by some Americans. It was a stopping place, store, and post office, all in one. The old father was a typical Yankee, and, like so many Americans, had knocked about all over the world. His boyhood had been spent at sea, and there were few European and American ports unknown to him: then, when the Franco-Prussian war broke out, he had volunteered and had served with the Zouaves through the siege of Sedan. A few years ago, he and his family of six strapping boys had moved into Alberta, come north-west of Edmonton, and now owned about a thousand acres of land between them. Pretty rough cards! Not caring much for God or man, but good

[1] *Cf.* p. 96 for further explanation of country school system.

farmers, and eventually perhaps good Canadians. Why not?

Next morning, I plodded on, though more slowly, as I was getting very footsore. After some six miles I heard the ringing sound of an axe a few hundred yards from the trail. Turning in to see who it was, I soon caught sight of a tent, and not far off two men, apparently father and son, hard at work "clearing" their land. The younger was cutting down trees, undergrowth, and every obstruction, and the elder was gathering it together into huge piles ready for burning; the green logs would have to dry out for months before they would burn, and the stumps would either be left to rot, which takes some years, or else would be pulled out with block and tackle and oxen; it means hard work before bush is converted into prairie. The homesteader earns his farm many times over before it is his. These two men were English; the son had been working on a farm in Manitoba for three years, gaining experience; a few months ago he had been joined by his father. They had heard there was good land in this part of the country; and, having found a homestead which suited them, had come right on to it and set to work. Next year the mother and sister are coming out, when there will be a shack ready for them, a garden, and several head of stock. Even so, they will have a hundred miles to travel in a wagon drawn by a team of oxen over bad trails. As a matter of fact, for mud-holes oxen are better than horses. Oxen spread their toes out as they plunge into the mud, and draw them in as they drag their feet out. They may only make 2 or 2½ miles an hour, but they can live on hay and need no oats.

These men were both keen Churchmen, and were surprised and pleased at the Church for once putting in an appearance in good time. The father had been forty years a Sunday-school teacher in London, and I hope we shall be able to make his shack a centre for services. They are poor, as indeed are most of the homesteaders in this part of Alberta. I know men who, when they first took up land, have had to borrow the ten dollars for the Government fee.

The Government demands that each man should live six months in each year, for three consecutive years, on his homestead, and have a certain number of acres "broken" (ploughed) before the land actually becomes his property and he is granted his "patent." What one finds over and over again is that, for the other six months in the year, the homesteader is forced to go off into the towns or the construction camps or the logging camps, and work for wages, so that he can live the rest of the year on his land.

By noon I found myself in a large settlement, and first visited the post office. The country here has been settled up over eight years, and, except for a short visit from a Presbyterian student, there has never been any official representative of religion in the place. There are over fifty separate homesteads, some being occupied by married people with large families. The post office is kept by some kind people called Peters; they live in a loghouse, half of which is the post office and a small store, the other half the living room, while a bedroom and kitchen are built out behind. They have contrived to make the living room very English in appearance; with mats on the floor, chintz-covered furniture, and geraniums in the windows. People are very clever out here. Necessity is the mother of invention. A well-made packing-case covered with cloth makes a nice piece of furniture; old barrels cut down, and suitably covered, make excellent arm-chairs; jam tins first-rate flower-pots, and cotton reels fine door-knobs.

After dinner, with the postmaster and his wife, I started off visiting. Let me give you a few impressions of the kind of people I met and stayed with. They are typical of those to be found in any young settlement out West.

The missionary, or "preacher," as he is almost always called, is received with wonderful hospitality and friendliness, though one could not help noticing that with many there is a feeling that in this rough country, where they have been forced to do without so many of the civilising influences of life, religion also is a luxury that can be equally well dispensed with. Is it to be wondered at, when one remembers how long they have been left without it? People, who in more civilised climes were probably good church-goers and sent their children to Sunday-school, have now long since got absolutely out of the way of going to any place of worship on Sunday.

They are not very clear about the differences between various religious bodies, or if they were so in other lands, they have not carried any party feeling out here. The one great difference they make is between "Protestant" and "Catholic." Most of the people would, I think, attend a service given by any Protestant "preacher." "We are all going the same way" is the constantly expressed opinion. This view, often the result of indifference and a good deal of ignorance, has its advantages and disadvantages.

One afternoon I called on an elderly couple who had only come out this spring from London. They were living in a minute shack, just one room; two beds, arranged one above the other like berths, occupied one side of the cabin; a table, cook-stove, chairs, and a couple of trunks took up most of the room on the other. They were Church people, and we had a long talk. When I rose to leave, it was getting dark. They wished to curtain off part of the room and let me sleep there. Of course I refused, but begged the use of a lean-to where there was some hay. They consented, and lent me some blankets. As the place was not properly covered, and there was rain in the air, I was glad of a piece of old tarpaulin, which stretched from one wall to the other and made a kind of tent. After making a "smudge"—a small fire of green twigs and bark, which only gives off smoke and keeps away the mosquitoes, I crept under the canvas and tried to sleep. But the mosquitoes were so bad, in spite of the smudge, that I welcomed the morning.

My host and hostess struck me as being extraordinarily sporting. He was a man of fifty, and had been for years a clerk in London. A bad throat had made an open-air life essential, and here they were in the wilds after many years of suburban life. They are building a larger house, and have three grown-up sons with them, but at present they are undergoing a good many hardships, and very cheerfully too! A great deal is heard of the prosperity of the homesteader; his life is painted in rosy colours. We see him sitting behind a fine team of horses reaping his gigantic crop of wheat in the golden rays of the setting sun. That is the traditional poster, and it deceives many.

What happens in scores of cases is this.

A man and his family scrape together enough money to come out here. They arrive in

Edmonton with just enough capital to buy a wagon, a team of oxen, a cook-stove, and a good store of provisions, and have a little money over for the first few months. The man finds suitable land—often a very expensive job through unscrupulous land-guides. If the man is sensible he will only take a qualified Government land-guide. They arrive at their homestead. It is just a piece of uncleared bush; they even have difficulty in determining its exact boundaries. There is certain to be a good deal of muskeg [1] on it, a few bad sloughs and a superfluity of trees. When cleared it will be as good agricultural land as any in Canada.

The man sets to work and gets up a shack. The family move in. They have their cook-stove; there is no difficulty about firewood. They have flour, pork, and potatoes, and thus they live. The man cuts down more logs, builds a barn, does some fencing and clears a large patch. The first year he makes nothing, but manages to keep himself and his family on the little capital still remaining. With the second year comes the pinch. The money is getting low, and still nothing coming in. The land is partially clear, and they have had a small crop of oats which they cannot get threshed, as a threshing machine could never be brought in over such

[1] A swamp of decayed vegetable matter, which has no foundation. It is often dangerous, and always troublesome to cross.

trails. But it is useful as feed for their cow and calf. The man is forced to go off and work for wages to keep the wolf from the door. The wife is left alone with the children. Finally, after many anxieties and hardships, they manage to fulfil the homestead conditions and "prove up" —that is, get their patent. Then the place is theirs, and they can do what they like with it. If a railway comes in, the land will go up in value, and they will probably be tempted to sell.

I think very few settlers really understand what they are coming to. Imagine a woman, who has spent most of her life in a semi-detached villa in some suburban street, her knowledge of farming confined to a few chickens in the back garden, her chief duty the supervision of a general servant, suddenly pitchforked out here, with everything to do for herself, no near neighbours, but days and weeks of loneliness. No wonder at first she is miserable. Many of the women, if they had the means, would return to England after a few weeks of this Western country; but it is wonderful to see how soon, in most cases, they "cotton" to the new conditions of life, and become so attached to the West that nothing would tempt them home to stay.

One day I went several miles to call on some people named Hind. As I rode up to the log-house, which stood on rising ground commanding a beautiful view, there came out of the house a middle-aged woman; tall, strong, and active she looked, as she leaned against the door shading her eyes with her hand. I introduced myself.

"So you've come at last!" she said, with tears in her eyes. "Six years we've been here, and never one sight of a preacher. This is just a great country, and we're doing fine; but no schooling for the children, that's what has been bothering me. Now we will have a regular Sunday-school and regular services."

"Only once a month, I fear, at present. It will be impossible to get round more often. You've been here six years?"

"Yes, before that we were in Wales. Why, my man—he only talks Welsh. I had a boarding-house near some big golf links, and was doing pretty well, but we came out for the children's sake. And now we have forty head of stock and close on five hundred acres between us. But there's been no school for the two young children. Why no school? Well, I think it is really because some of 'em don't want one; it means taxes. And the bachelors—well, they're none too keen."

I suggested giving the children some Bible pictures.

"Why, sure, put your horse in the barn and come right in. You're not going any farther to-day. Now don't you say anything. There's always room here for the parson. Why, King

George himself wouldn't have the parson's bed!"

So there I stayed, and had a delightful time with these strong Welsh Church people, learning to know the grown-up boys, teaching the children and reading to the mother—good, hospitable soul that she was. They all came to the service on Sunday.

I stayed Saturday night with a bachelor called Sheldon—a Canadian and a Presbyterian. The interior of the shacks out here are very much the same. This particular shack was about sixteen feet broad and twenty-four feet long; the walls were logs chinked with mud, the floor and the roof boarded, the latter vaulted and covered with rubberoid. In one corner stood the cook-stove with its tin piping going out through a hole in the roof; it burnt wood and contained a good-sized oven, and was arranged with holes in the top for saucepans and frying-pans. The crockery and pans not being in use hung from nails knocked into the logs. In the centre was the table, covered with dirty enamel tea things; a few old chairs and boxes formed the seating accommodation. In one corner was an old packing-case, on which stood a tin basin for washing, and a bucket containing drinking water, and in it a "dipper." A dipper is not unlike a small enamel saucepan, and is used as a cup. Everybody as they come in from work takes a long pull at the dipper. People get into the habit of consuming great quantities of water. In another corner was a double bed made of boards nailed to the logs; on it were some rather dirty blankets and an ancient-looking pillow. Near by stood the inevitable trunk, in which were a few clothes and other treasures. On the log walls were some gaudy pictures, mostly advertisements of implement companies, and opposite the door hung a rifle, a shot-gun, and two knives. I found my friend frying some bacon and potatoes on the cook-stove, a little taciturn and melancholy.

"Say, parson, it's fierce this 'baching.' If a fellow cooks properly, he's less time for his work outside, and if he doesn't cook properly he'll likely take sick. So you're going to hold a meeting here to-morrow, eh?"

"That's what I want," I said. "But the trails are so bad I guess there won't be many."

"Well, there'll sure be plenty of excuses, though bad trails won't keep 'em from a dance, if they want to come. Put your horse in the barn and give him a feed, and then come and have a bite yourself."

After supper we lit our pipes, and I drew on my host to relate his experiences in the Klondyke rush—a marvellous story, far more interesting than many a novel. And then after I had read from the Bible we retired to the same bunk. Personally, I passed an uncomfortable night

The bunk sloped towards the middle, and I was continually bumping against my host, who, besides gaining possession of most of the blankets, had an unpleasant but common habit of spitting upon the floor. This he did with remarkable frequency, but, fortunately for me, with tolerable accuracy.

Indeed, some of the bachelors out here seem to "pig" it in the most horrible way. Yesterday I came across a funny old Yankee. He had just taken up a homestead, though almost sixty-five years of age. He lived in quite the dirtiest shack I have ever seen. It really was filthy, and so was he. I could hardly get in because of the cattle which stood almost inside the door. The shack was small and dark, and under the bed were a number of hens. We had a chat, but I was thankful to be able to say I had had dinner, as I watched him begin to cook something—Heaven knows what—with hands which were absolutely black.

We had the service next day; nominally at 3 P.M. But time is arbitrary. Everybody has his own, and it is always different from his neighbour's. But by 3.30 over twenty had assembled. They sat all round the shack on improvised benches, and we had a shortened form of Evensong. Many of them were not Church people, and were unfamiliar with the service, but with the help of those excellent little S.P.C.K. books, and a few explanations now and then, they joined in well, and seemed to like it. We had several hymns, though one learns by experience there are not more than six or eight we all know well enough to sing unaccompanied. "Nearer, my God, to Thee," "Rock of Ages," "Jesu, Lover of my Soul," and "Abide with Me" are great stand-byes. The service was a little interrupted by the fact that our host, having his week's bread in the oven, kept peeping at it to see it did not burn.

We probably should have had more people but for two reasons: first, the bad trails, and secondly, the general prejudice which most people have against going to a "meeting" (as they call it) at a private house. Very often they imagine they are dire enemies with the person in whose shack the service is to be held, or else they are afraid they will meet some family there with whom they are not on speaking terms. You have no idea of the amount of backbiting and slander there is in many of these country communities, where almost every nationality, social class, and variety of religious belief is represented. Bitter feuds arise from the most petty reasons—a fenced-in trail, a poisoned dog, straying pigs, refusal to lend a plough. Things such as these will cause two families half a mile from each other to live for months or even years as irreconcilable enemies, and too often the whole settlement is dragged into siding with one party or the other. I do not wish to generalise. *All* districts are *not* like this. There are not a few shining exceptions. But many of them are undoubtedly quarrelsome. The people have little to feed their minds on. They do not appear to read anything except possibly a weekly paper and Eaton's Catalogue.

For this reason, if for none other, it is essential to get up a church as soon as possible. Failing that, we generally try to get a school or store or some common meeting place. I had a service in a store the other day. The people sat on two benches in the middle of the shop, and I stood behind the counter. The shelves, which covered every wall, were stocked with groceries, axes, tools, clothes, and boots, while the ceiling was hung with pots and pans. When I stood up to speak I was surrounded by slabs of bacon, sacks of flour, and all the other paraphernalia which a general store in a more or less uncivilised country is expected to supply. It is not very church-like, and always results in extensive Sunday trading directly the service is over. On this occasion the storekeeper was an old Cambridge blue; he went round afterwards, and collected the offertory on the lid of a box.

The rain continued almost unintermittently on this trip, and I didn't have dry clothes on for ten days. On my thirty-mile walk back to Mosside

I was soon wet through, and plunged through everything, regardless of mud, water, and muskeg. The water had gone down a little within the ten days, but in several places it was necessary to wade above the waist in water for two or three hundred yards. At Hilton's my coloured friend again took me across in a boat. The mail wagon had just gone on as I arrived, having taken four hours to get across. The mailman took the mail across in the boat, swam the horses, and then made them pull the wagon bodily through the water at the end of a logging chain.

I slept at Hilton's, and next morning overtook the mail. Arriving at the Little Paddle about noon, I found the team and mail wagon standing by the side of the swollen creek. The driver was scouting along the bank to find some place to cross. I was in the same predicament, as the bridge which had carried me across before was now too high out of the water to move. But at this moment up came the mailman with a French Canadian, whom he had discovered two miles down the river. The French Canadian had a boat, and we drove down to his shack, where we had some pork and eggs for dinner. Then we took the mail bags, and our host, having rowed us down the river about half a mile in his very rickety boat, landed us safely the other side.

A KENTISH FARMER S NEW HOME
(Log shack lined with newspapers)

INDIAN'S GRAVE IN THE BUSH NEAR MARLBORO

The mail carrier and I then shouldered as many of the bags as we could, and carried them the remaining mile into Mosside. Thus His Majesty's mail reached the end of the first stage of its journey.

I caught Charlie, and rode the remaining twenty-five miles back here to Lac la Nonne, with no further incident except that I overtook an Indian pack train.

Imagine a string of Indian ponies, stretching perhaps nearly half a mile—some with packs on their backs, and some carrying the squaws and children—the men leading them or walking by their sides. The squaws were dressed in red and other bright-coloured blankets—their babies either slung on their backs behind, or propped on the saddle in front. The pack ponies were heavily laden with tents and clothes and camping utensils. Most of the women carried their husbands' guns slung on the shoulder as well as the babies! The squaws carried on conversation, shouting from one to the other in guttural tones. The men, in much less interesting dress, plodded along silently, except when the ponies needed some encouragement over a particularly bad mud-hole. They had come south from the Athabasca, and were heading for Lake St. Anne, where they will sell the furs which they have spent the winter in procuring. They made a most picturesque scene, as they wound along through the trees in the evening sunlight. I rode past the whole line, and as I reached the head of the procession they were just turning off the trail into a bunch of spruce trees, where was to be their camping ground for the night.

SETTLERS AT HOME

LAC LA NONNE, ALBERTA,
Sept. 22nd.

I LEFT here on horseback two weeks ago on my usual monthly round, travelling every day, and staying almost every night in a different place. Having arranged to meet Mr. Boyd at Onoway, I started due south from here across Rich Valley, and then through many miles of heavy timber and thick brush. It was a lonely ride, but as I got near Onoway there were more signs of life. Onoway is 40 miles due west of Edmonton and will be the junction of the Canadian Northern Transcontinental main line and Peace River branch of the same Company.

To the uninitiated, the whole work of railroad construction in this country is a marvel. First, the small party of experienced engineers, who decide roughly on the best route; then the survey parties, who run the line through the bush, putting in stakes to guide those who come after. Then the right-of-way cutters, who cut down and burn the timber and brush to a width of a hundred feet. Then comes the main work of "grading," "exalting the valleys and bringing low the mountains and hills," on the principle of "cut and fill." This work is let out by the Company on contract. The bridging of innumerable creeks and rivers, and the building of long stretches of trestle across particularly low-lying land, take time, money, and skill, and then finally comes the laying of the steel. It is always inspiring suddenly to come out on the "right of way," perhaps after travelling many miles through thickly timbered and sparsely settled country, and to look right up and down the avenue, silent and deserted; no grading has been done, and the ground rises and falls just in its natural state; stumps project out of the long thick grass, while here and there are stretches of muskeg and pools of water. In a few months the whole scene will be changed. The avenue will have become a long level stretch of heaped up "dirt"; bridges will have been constructed and steel laid, while any moment a construction train may come lurching along over the newly laid line. What the coming of the railroad means to the people, how much speculation there is as to where the station and the town-site will be put, how eagerly every detail is discussed, you will readily understand.

It was the day of the first annual fair ever held at Onoway, and, to celebrate the occasion, free meals for all who came were provided by the hospitable ladies of the settlement. The judging of horses, cattle, and pigs was in full swing when

I arrived, and was followed by pony races, foot races, and all kinds of sports. The brilliant weather had brought together a good crowd. It was much like a rural gathering in the old country, though the round red faces, typical of English farmers, were hardly so noticeable as the hard keen features of the Western Americans and Canadians. We have a Church and Mission House at Onoway. Mercer (late of Leeds) is in charge of it, and holds services at various points in a large district.

I met Mr. Boyd, and we left fairly late in the evening, riding about twelve miles by the light of the moon to Lac St. Anne—a very old settlement, where there has been a Hudson Bay Station for many years. We stayed with the Hudson Bay factor and his wife, who received us most kindly.

Next morning, we had not travelled many miles before we met a fellow galloping along the trail at a tremendous pace. He drew rein when he reached us.

"Say, is there a doctor at St. Anne?"

"No, I don't think so. I guess you'll have to go on to Wabamun."

"Gee whiz! that's another twelve miles, I guess."

"Anything serious?"

"I should say! Fellow fifteen miles up country shot himself. Only a proper doctor can help; guess leg'll have to come off."

And off he went. North-west of Edmonton there are no proper doctors, and no nurses for the country districts.

About mid-day we came to the Narrows—a perfect spot. The water of the lake, which here narrows to about seventy yards, sparkled in the sun. On the other side of the channel was an Indian encampment, with its picturesque tepees (Indian tents). The ferry, worked by hand, was slowly bringing across a wagon and team. The trees were as fresh and green as in springtime, after the heavy rains of this summer.

Our mid-day meal we had with a former officer in the British Army, and supper at a stopping place kept by a fellow who was once manager of a department in a large West-end shop in London.

Long after it had got dark we came to the Pembina, where there is a stopping place kept by an American family called Hudson. A group of loghouses comprising bunkhouse, kitchen and eating-house, and two barns, stood on the bank of the river. Old Mr. Hudson, who reminded us of St. Peter in face, but in no other way as far as I can remember, bade us welcome; and Mr. Boyd and I, having seen to our horses, sat warming ourselves at the heater in the bunk-house. The nights in September begin to get chilly.

Old Hudson chuckled.

"Well, I guess you don't have roads like this in England, eh? Some of you fellows from over there find this Western country kind of hard, I guess? Believe me, an awful bunch get stung over this homesteading. A fellow's got to hustle a bit if he's going to make good in this blamed country." And he spat on the floor.

We agreed.

"Why, there's a fellow three miles from here on the trail, other side of the river. He's right out from London, England, and he don't hardly know an ox from a horse. He's taken ten days to make that three miles. Believe me, he's a crackerjack, that fellow! Why, if he don't get a move on, he'll be froze up there, and never get his blamed outfit out of the mud this year. You'll see him for yourselves to-morrow. Give him a bit of advice, and tell him to make tracks out of this country. He'll never do any good anyway."

I asked him what he thought of Englishmen as a whole, as I had been told only the other day by a homestead inspector that they picked up the new conditions as well as anyone.

"Why, if you get hold of the right sort, who'll stay with the job and see the thing through, they'll have as dandy a farm as any of us. And I know plenty of 'em who have, too. But so many of 'em think this Western country's a snap, and it isn't—and then when they're down and out through their own blamed fault, they're the first to knock[1] the country."

"What do you think of the country yourself?"

"Oh, not too bad! We've got good water, plenty of firewood, and it's a good stock-raising country. A fellow can soon clear enough land to raise feed, and when we get a railway we'll be all right. Still, a homesteader's not making much money at present—about as much as a preacher, I guess?" he added with a wink.

Everyone in the West is out to make every red cent they can, and the preacher is almost always considered to be on the same quest.

"But we didn't come out West to make a pile!"

"Well, I guess you didn't, either. I'll tell you right now, if a fellow could buy a through ticket to Heaven there'd be an awful bunch of third-class passengers!"

About ten o'clock Mr. Boyd and I retired, which meant climbing into a double bunk full of hay and rolling ourselves up in a couple of blankets—rather different from a bedroom at Lambeth, I suggested, this loghouse in the West, the stars shining through chinks in the walls, the floor rough and well spat upon, and old Hudson snoring in the corner.

Next morning we breakfasted soon after six o'clock, and having heard that there was a family

[1] *i.e.* disparage.

about a mile off, who had four children to be christened, we started off on foot. We soon found the place, and having introduced ourselves received a warm welcome. They were American people. The good woman bustled about, spread a white cloth on the table, got a bowl of water, and explained the names of all the children, some of which were wonderful. The elder daughters bustled the children into clean clothes in a marvellously short time, and scrubbed their faces. When all was ready, Mr. Boyd took the baptism.

"How much do you charge for doing them?" the parents asked (as if they had just been vaccinated), and seemed surprised at learning there was no charge. If they wished to give something, they could help the Mission by giving some small sum, which would go, as do all such occasional contributions, to our Holiday Fund. We have two weeks' holidays in the summer, and each man has a grant of fifteen dollars (£3) towards it.[1]

They undoubtedly entered into the meaning

[1] The theory of the Mission is that a man should receive a bare living wage. He has all expenses of board and lodging and travelling met from the general fund, and receives in addition ten dollars (£2) a month for clothes and personal expenses. Clergy and laymen all receive the same. Towards the expenses of the Mission every parish is urged to contribute. The chief part of the money required for its support is provided by the Archbishops' Western Canada Fund in England, but each year the amount subscribed locally has increased; in 1910 these local subscriptions amounted to 254 dollars, in 1911 to 750 dollars, in 1912 to 2073 dollars, and in 1913 to 2600 dollars.

of the service, and I hope will fulfil their part of the agreement, and teach the children something, if only the rudiments, of religion. In a month or two I shall try to start a Sunday-school there.

Hudson never charged us a cent for ourselves or our horses, and was kindness itself. We crossed the river in his ferry, and very soon came to the daft Englishman. The trail was certainly fearful—two feet of mud, without exaggeration—but a good team, with not too heavy a load, should have been able to get through all right. The fellow seemed utterly dazed and stupid, a little queer in the head, I think. He had "cached" (*i.e.* hidden) half his load in the bush, and the other half made quite a small load for his huge team of oxen. For the team he had paid two hundred and fifty dollars, which is quite a large sum, but I think they were worth it, and they ought to have pulled him and the whole of his load from Edmonton to his destination (a distance of about a hundred and thirty miles) in about a week. Evidently he was quite incapable of driving oxen. To get the best work out of them you must understand them. Bad language is a *sine quâ non*—the oxen understand it! Certainly they are most exasperating animals—and if one did not actually use bad language, one would be obliged to invent some alternative equally soothing to the feelings. We asked him where he was going, and he told us that he had never seen his homestead, but that he believed it was surrounded by muskeg, and that he would have the greatest difficulty in reaching it at all. He seemed averse to receiving any help from people passing, and he is now a perfect laughing-stock on the road. He had a small cow tied on behind, which was for ever getting loose, and he would spend hours looking for it. He seemed obstinate as well as stupid. We gave him friendly advice, and told some men about him when we reached Roydale, but even if they go back and offer help, I doubt whether he will accept it.

As a matter of fact, I heard yesterday, on my way home, what happened. On arriving at his homestead, he gave up all hope of making anything of it, and sold up his whole outfit. He had given two hundred and fifty dollars for his oxen—he now parted with the oxen, a new wagon, a new plough, and a new cook-stove, all for two hundred and twenty dollars. People fleeced him, seeing they had a soft thing. The man was of course a little daft, otherwise he could not have been such a consummate fool.

As a matter of fact, English people do far better out here than they usually get credit for. Their farms are generally just as prosperous and well managed as those of their Canadian or American neighbours. They are often accused of being too keen on shooting and of neglecting their homesteads for sport, but that is nonsense. It must be remembered that the Englishman starts with a tremendous handicap if compared to the American, who has lived all his life in the Western States, where agricultural conditions are very similar to those prevailing here. The Englishman is generally quite as well educated, though not, perhaps, so "cute" as his Western neighbours.

The idea of many of the more poorly educated Canadians and Americans about England is simply ludicrous—they judge its importance by its size. "Why, you've got to wait till the tide goes down before you can turn a four-horse team!" as a Canadian once said to me. They think that there is not much work to be had there, and that if a man is to live decently he must emigrate, whereas I would *never* advise a man to leave even a tolerably good job in the old country without very careful consideration. They seem sometimes to look upon England as a little island built all over with bricks and mortar down to the water's edge, where nobody has room to move. Many of them have knocked about all over the States and Canada, doing all kinds of jobs in a way impossible in a country where there is not more work than workers, but of any really old settled country they have not the least idea, nor, it seems to me, do they really understand what naval and military power means.

We reached Greencourt that night, and, next day being Sunday, Mr. Boyd had a Celebration of the Holy Communion in the morning in a private house, kindly lent for the purpose, and in the afternoon there was a service in the store, at which he preached; there were quite a good number. Next day we went on to the Peavine country, visiting at various homesteads on the way. The following morning Mr. Boyd started on his way back to Lac la Nonne, and then farther east. He is travelling over the whole province of the Mission, so as to get a really good idea of problems and needs.

I have met quite a number of Socialists out here—or shall I say extremely strong Radicals? One afternoon I visited a shack owned by a tall, husky, strong, muscular Canadian.

"I'm a bit of a Socialist," he said almost as soon as I had got inside. "What's your opinion?"

For answer I produced a little book called *The History of Socialism*, which I happened to have in my pocket.

"Gee whiz! But that's fine! You must be keen, to carry that about with you!" he replied, and thereupon looked upon me as a brother—a conclusion which I fear subsequent conversation showed him was a little premature. Like many of these men he was very keen on his subject, but poorly educated. Socialism does not seem to have much of a chance in the West, where everybody, if he works, can soon acquire his own hundred and sixty acres in the country, or his own lot and house in the town. There is one settlement which either Whitaker or I visit every month, where lives one of the leaders of Western Socialism, John Kaye by name. More hospitable and kind to us no man could be. But he is extremely bitter against society as at present ordered, and religion—and many is the argument we have had.

Two days later the shack of my Socialist friend was burnt to the ground. He was out "clearing," saw a big smoke, and rushed back in time to see his little frame-house a mass of flames. He could get nothing out, and in a few minutes he was the proud possessor of the overalls, shirt, and boots in which he stood. The settlement got up a dance for him—twenty-five cents entrance, and the food supplied gratis by the ladies. Though there is a good deal of "ugly" talking, people are wonderfully kind to each other when it comes to practical help in time of trouble.

On Tuesday afternoon I went to visit some delightful Norwegians, who asked me to baptize their baby. As I knew no clergyman would be round for months, I consented. Their shack was rather rough—the log walls plastered with old Scandinavian newspapers which were beginning to peel off, and the roof just bare poplar poles and moss, which, to judge from the scuffling, must have been the home of many mice. Inside I found the grandmother looking after the baby. She was an old woman with yellow wizened skin, and an orange-coloured handkerchief tied over her head; between her lips was an old pipe, and she kept puffing evil-smelling tobacco from her mouth as she crooned over the baby, a spittoon at her side. They decided they would like to have the baby baptized that very day, and great preparations began. The father got into his Sunday clothes, and went off to find godparents, who proved to be two bachelors from neighbouring homesteads. His wife bustled about and prepared dinner. The old grandmother scrubbed the floor, and did a general clearing up. The baby was washed and dressed in clean clothes, and then I had to get the name of the boy, which the mother pronounced so badly that at first I thought it must be some unpronounceable Norwegian word, and wondered how I should get through it at the service.

Then the godfathers arrived, and I got their names and those of the parents all written with much difficulty and hesitation. Dinner came next, in two batches—the table was rather small, and we could not all sit down together—and finally, when all was cleared away, and the womenkind had also got into their Sunday clothes, I did what I was beginning to think I never should do, and that was baptize the baby, who, I may say, behaved very creditably.

They did not appear to show any interest as to what religious body I belonged, if only it was Protestant. One question, and one alone, the mother had asked me about myself.

"You're not a Catholic, I guess?" she said with a sharp look. Of course I knew she meant Roman Catholic, and simply said "No."

"Well, I'm glad of that," she replied, "because I wouldn't like to have a child of mine done by a Catholic."

"That's right," joined in her husband, "as long as you're not a Catholic, it's all one to me what you belong to."

This rather depressing broad-mindedness is typical of Western religious life.

There are a great number of Norwegians and Swedes homesteading through the North-West country. The Teutonic element, namely, German, Danish, Dutch, and Scandinavian, is a valuable asset to Canada. They are excellent settlers and generally fine axemen, being used to the woods.

That night I slept with a funny old man who had red underclothing, over which—it being a cold night—he put his white nightshirt. In this garb he knelt down and said his prayers—it was rather nice, but looked very queer.

A "STOPPING-PLACE" AND ITS PROPRIETORS

BUILDING LAC LA NONNE CHURCH

THE MAIL CARRIER

I wonder with how many different people I have slept in the same bed on this last journey!

The following day I spent in trying to organise a Sunday-school in a district only recently settled. But already the people have been enterprising enough to form a school district, elect trustees, build the school, and engage the teacher. I wanted to organise a Sunday-school as well, and find teachers to take charge of it, as I knew that my already large district would preclude my getting there on a Sunday myself. Everybody had to be visited within a couple of days. Nearly all were friendly, but one old Methodist couple were rather cold. The old woman had been described to me as "dry as dust and ready to blow away," and certainly she was a wizened old thing, with not an ounce of romance about her. I called—was invited in, and asked to sit down.

"So you're Church, are you? Well, my husband and I would rather have a good Methodist but——"

"I guess you'll have to make me do," I finished for her. She half smiled; "Beggars can't be choosers anyway," she said, "and you're better than no one. When are you going to have Sunday-school?"

"For the first time on Friday in the school, and afterwards every Sunday if I can find the teachers."

"Well, it's a good thing to teach the kids anyway. You'll stay and have some dinner?"

I accepted, and we had a good talk; she never thawed out much on the question of religion. She was an American Methodist, disliked our form of service, hated our government by Bishops, which offended her sense of democracy, and thought that we were not far from Rome because she had been to a church where the clergyman wore a surplice.

There can be no doubt that it is far *easier* to hold an emotional service, consisting of sentimental hymns, long *ex tempore* prayers, and fervid preaching. But the dignified liturgy of the Church of England, if somewhat shortened and simplified, soon becomes popular with a congregation of the most varied type. A large number of immigrants who come to Canada from England belong to the Anglican Church. Of those who come from Scotland, the majority are Presbyterian, while a vast number of the farmers who come from over the border are adherents of Methodism, or claim to belong to some unheard of sect.

Among others I looked up the teacher, quite a young fellow, who had only been out a few weeks from England. He earns about sixty-five dollars (that is £13) a month, out of which he has to pay about twenty dollars (£4) for board and lodging. Having learnt that I had the permission of the three trustees, he readily put the school at my disposal at 3.30 on Friday afternoon; and so I turned up at that time and took the school over from him. Any child who wished could leave, but none did. We started by standing for the Lord's Prayer, of which they were completely ignorant. I told them a little about the childhood of Christ, and ended up by giving them each a picture. They all departed evidently meaning to come again.

Before leaving the settlement, I arranged with two capable women to take over the teaching on the following Sunday. It was difficult, because people are fearfully jealous of each other out here. I think if I had to name the cardinal fault of these Western communities, I should say it was jealousy. Both men and women seem to dislike seeing anyone doing better than themselves, and immediately begin to attribute their success to dishonesty or some other absolutely false reason.

On Saturday night I was the guest of one of the most curious men I have ever known in this country. I met him on the trail not far from his house, and he asked me to stay the night with him. My host was a huge Irishman of six foot three or four, holding himself as straight as a Guardsman; a well-trimmed pointed beard and moustache gave him an almost French appearance, an impression still further strengthened by his beautiful manners and quiet refined voice. He dispensed hospitality in his loghouse with all the old-world courtesy of a French nobleman, and offered liver and bacon and tea as if it had been the most *recherché* dish and choicest wine. The house, of which the log walls were covered with a kind of whitewash, consisted of three rooms, which were hung with old family portraits, here a General or Admiral with the wig and uniform of a century ago, there an eighteenth century belle or grande dame of times gone by; interspersed were paintings of Indians and other drawings. A few easy-chairs stood round the stove; the floor was bare; from the rafters hung some saddlery and unwashed clothes; blankets and sacks of flour occupied various corners. Bachelor's quarters all right—but with an air of refinement about it all, unusual in this wild woolly West!

After supper we had a delightful time. My host goes almost every year to the Peace River country prospecting. He knew this Western country in the old days of the big ranches; he served in the South African War, and told me that on the voyage out the Canadians were seldom heard to pass any remarks about things nautical. They were up against something quite unfamiliar to them, and therefore they kept silence and drank everything in.

On Sunday I only had two services, but some miles to travel from one to the other. It would leave me little time for dinner, did not a friend, who lives midway between the two settlements, always have something absolutely ready, so that

I can look in, take a bite, and go straight on. On this occasion he was out, but two saucepans were steaming on the stove, one labelled "beef," the other "musk-rat *à la mode*." Some people eat musk-rat out here, but personally I disliked it, and ate the beef.

On Monday morning Bury (a fire-ranger, who has a homestead in the district) and I started off from the Peavine fire-ranging. Every fire-ranger has a certain district which he has to patrol at various seasons of the year—chiefly of course the spring and the fall. If there is a big forest fire he is entitled to call out all the nearest settlement to fight it. This year the danger is small—it has been too wet. Every day Bury is out fire-ranging, he makes about four dollars (that is 16*s.*) a day. Like so many other appointments—for instance, post office, land office, homestead and road inspectorships—fire-ranging is a Government job, and if the Government changes Bury is likely to lose his post.

We took a pack pony, and I was shown how to throw the diamond hitch, quite a complicated business if you don't know how. On one side of the pack saddle was the tent rolled up: on the other, blankets and waterproof sheet; in the middle, a sack containing bread, potatoes, salt, &c. Stuck on the top we had a frying-pan and an axe. He carried a big rifle, and I a "twenty-two." We also had a revolver. The weather was fine, but a horribly cold wind blew from the north-west. We struck right away across country into the teeth of this wind, and after four or five miles had left all settlement behind and were in the bush—passing now through stretches of burnt poplar country, and now through valleys dark with spruce and undergrowth. At mid-day we camped by a creek and rested an hour. By 5 P.M. we had reached our camping ground about two miles short of the Athabasca.

So far there had been a very rough trail made by the surveying party, who were through this country two years ago; between us and the river, a distance of two miles, there was a pack trail which I found it extremely hard to detect, the ground being covered with dead leaves. Our camping ground was very ideally situated. We found ourselves in a most delightful dell, which would have satisfied even the Romany Rye; on three sides of us a steep bank, on the other a precipitous slope downwards into a dark ravine full of spruce trees, at the bottom of which gurgled a stream of clear water.

We unpacked, tethered out the horse, got a fire lighted, cooked potatoes, and put up the tent. By the time we were squatting round the camp fire and the potatoes were frizzling in the frying-pan, the sky was brilliant with stars and the Northern Lights lit up the whole heaven. As I lay on the ground puffing away at my pipe and looked into the glowing logs, our little camp seemed quite perfect.

We hoped to get a moose or a bear—but we never got nearer than seeing their tracks. The partridges and prairie chickens (called fool hens from their stupid habit of sitting on the branches waiting to be shot) were pretty numerous, and rabbits too. We slaughtered sufficient to make us a good "bouillon," as Bury expressed it—the said bouillon being a hotch-potch of everything thrown into a billy and boiled over the fire. The night was cold and windy.

Next morning we left camp, and started off for the Athabasca. In a line it was two miles—but it must have been far longer through the thick bush—consisting of huge spruce trees, many of which had fallen across our trail, Bury told me that the Athabasca was "pretty fine" at the point at which we should strike it, but I was certainly not prepared for the magnificence of the scene as we suddenly came right out on to the edge of a cliff, some two hundred feet high, at the foot of which rolled this magnificent Northern river. Its course was broken up by innumerable islands—some of which were so long and irregular that one got the impression of not one but many rivers threading their way among the hills. The whole scene lay before us like a map. One could have chucked a stone into the river below. The banks on the other side were not high, so the view towards the north was unimpeded; range after range of hills, covered with virgin forest, stretched away as far as the eye could reach. The formation of the river scenery reminded me rather of the Seine between Elbeuf and Rouen —but how much larger and more untamed these vast tracts of rough scrubby forest country looked than the rich green meadows of Normandy. It certainly was a noble view; nothing I have yet seen has given me such a sense of the grandeur of this magnificent Western Country. And people say there is no romance about the West!

We clambered down the cliff front. Bury, who is a magnificent shot, killed a duck, swimming many feet below in the river, with his rifle. It jumped out of the water, and flopped back again dead. We walked some distance along the sandy bank of the river, and saw the tracks of many animals who had been down to the water to drink. Back to our camp by 5 P.M. Supper and bed about 8.30. It was so cold that we pulled the tent down, and retired right underneath it. If one felt stuffy, one had only to pull back the tent and look right up into the stars.

By Wednesday evening we were back in the settlement. I spent the night at Bury's shack, but went that afternoon to visit a man who, I had just heard, was very ill—a young Canadian bachelor, twenty-seven years of age. I found him lying in his own shack, in the bed in which I had more than once slept with him. It was obvious at once that he was terribly ill, both lungs being affected. He was breathing quick and sharp, like a dog out of breath, and looked dreadfully weak There was a good woman looking after him—a neighbour—but I do not think she knew much about nursing. His illness must have been coming on for some time, and I remember now, when I stayed there, he was troubled by a suspicious cough.

He seemed pleased to see me, and smiled as I came in. It was most pathetic to see this fellow lying there in his little shack out in the Far West, miles from his parents, whom he had not seen for nine years—miles from all medical aid. He told me he did not think he would live many days, and asked me to pray for him. This I did, and also, at his request, read to him a little out of his own Bible. I cannot tell you how glad I was I could go and see him; but that evening I was forced to leave him, and start on my way back here. The establishment of country hospitals is a crying need all through this newly settled country, north-west of Edmonton. I think all our men would say the same. Nurses and doctors are badly wanted, and if the Church could do something to supply them, she would be surely performing a noble work.[1]

[1] *Cf.* page 256, for what the Mission has been able to do to meet this need.

P.S.—This letter, though finished long ago, could not be sent off till to-day. There are only two mails in and out a week. This morning I received word that Fortescue died not many hours after I left. The funeral is to-day. I only wish I could have been there to take it. One cannot help feeling that with proper medical aid he could easily have been saved.

"PACKING" THE MAIL IN A COUNTRY DISTRICT

THE AUTHOR STARTING ON A TWO WEEKS' ROUND
(45° below zero)

NEW CITIZENS OF CANADA

LAC LA NONNE, ALBERTA,
January 11th

WINTER is here with a vengeance, and we are in the middle of a cold snap ; not more than nine inches of snow, but the thermometer far below zero. Our house here is far from warm. We stoke the heater up with as much wood as it can carry—dry and green—before we turn in, but, even so, everything is frozen in the morning. It is not safe to leave water in the kettle or buckets, as it might burst them. The mere "hewing of wood and drawing of water," in other words "chores," under these conditions is a nuisance. Under ordinary circumstances Jim Clare takes a good deal off our hands, but he has been away for some days. First the fire has to be lit, then the water has to be thawed, likewise the bread, which is as hard as a brick, and the butter. I confess that visions of the shiny-faced Abbott (you remember my scout at Christ Church), bringing in eggs and bacon to a warm oak-panelled room in Peck, sometimes come floating before my eyes.

After breakfast the horses have to be watered at the ice-hole in the lake. The ice is forty-two inches thick, and the hole has to be chopped round with an axe every morning to keep it open. Then the horses must be fed and the barn cleaned out. Washing up and inside chores take some time. After Matins, we get some time for reading, while the potatoes and meat for dinner are thawing out in front of the stove. After dinner I helped Whitaker hitch up—he was off to see Confirmation candidates—and then set to to saw enough wood to last for the next twenty-four hours. Before it gets dark there is water to be fetched, the hens to be fed, and the horses to be seen to for the night, and then it is time to prepare supper.

But the winter is a glorious time—dry, bright and invigorating, like a Swiss winter, only far better. For driving we have long fur coats and caps with ear flaps. The fur is not expensive, but very warm and used by everyone. For riding (which is impossible in very cold weather) and for walking, a short sheepskin coat is best. For footwear either moccasins or felt boots are good. If there is an unexpected thaw, which is quite usual so near the mountains when a sudden chinook (warm wind) comes through from British Columbia, rubbers can be worn over them.

But nothing that I have ever experienced comes up to sleighing. To drive in a "jumper" over a frozen lake covered with snow, well wrapped in furs, behind a fast team of ponies with jingling bells, on a brilliant night with a full moon, is one of the most glorious and exhilarating experiences a man can have. From the horses' nostrils hang long icicles, which they try in vain to shake off by sneezing. If they sweat at all, their coat becomes covered with a kind of hoar frost. When hitching up, one must be careful to thaw out the steel bits indoors before putting them into the horses' mouths, or the steel will blister them. If any metal is touched with damp hands, or a nail put into the mouth for a second, the skin will come off. I found the ink in my fountain pen froze; also the nicotine in my pipe, unless I was careful to keep continually drawing.

These things sound rather trying, but one can work perfectly well in one's shirtsleeves if the sun is out, and two winters—if not exceptionally severe—are, in my opinion, far preferable to one summer with its rain and mosquitoes.

It is curious travelling over the old trails under the new conditions. One can now go high and dry over places which in summer are perfect nightmares. The bad muddy places in the timber are now the most pleasantly sheltered, and the open dry stretches which one had looked forward to in the summer are now the bleakest and most exposed parts of the journey. The rivers are all frozen, there is no ferryman to pay, and no time need be wasted if he does not happen to be there.

Let me tell you of the service held yesterday

for the first time in our new church at Lac la Nonne.

Huxtable, who was to preach at the opening, arrived at our place about 10 P.M. on Tuesday night, after a terribly cold journey. We never expected him to turn up so late, but he lost his way. We had arranged that the first service in the new church should be a Celebration of the Holy Communion next morning at 8 A.M. The church was not really finished, the walls consisting of only one thickness of lumber. As we walked across the lake yesterday morning, enveloped in our fur coats, before the sun came up, the thermometer was at fifty-nine degrees below zero. The little building was simply arctic when we struggled up the bank from the lake and opened the door. We ourselves were pretty cold. I rubbed my nose and chin almost continually while crossing the lake. Our eyelashes and eyebrows were white with frost, and of course our breath froze solid on the front of our coats and caps, and on our fur collars. We got a fire going, and for some time simply stood round it as we were, gradually warming. Though the church is small, yet the heater, which soon became red-hot, took a long time to make any appreciable difference to the temperature. I tried to persuade Whitaker to celebrate near the heater, but he preferred to go to the altar, and so stood at the east end of the building some distance from the wood fire. The wine and bread, both of which had become solid on our way across, had to be thawed out, and Whitaker left them by the heater until he came to the Prayer of Consecration. They would have frozen stiff in a few minutes had they been left on the altar. I think the wine was beginning to freeze again as we partook of it, and Whitaker's thumb was a little touched where he was holding the paten. He had been forced to come down and warm his hands in the middle of the service. Two women, who most bravely turned out on such a morning, turned faint with the coldness of their feet, but they managed to stay the service out.

In the afternoon we had another service, to which quite a number came, considering this unusually severe weather. However, it is good to feel that the winter is by no means harmful to the soil. The hard frosts retain the moisture which would otherwise drain away quickly, and the snow cannot melt at once, but disappears gradually, as the ground thaws out. I am told, however, that a foot of snow is only equivalent to an inch of rain, but I believe it is generally agreed that the winters are a blessing for the agricultural West.

There is a good deal of social life in these farming communities during the winter. Last week there was a dance in the schoolhouse.

Generally they are given to raise money for the school or the church. In the latter case the ladies of the settlement bring cakes and pastries, and any and everybody from far and near is welcome. The men generally pay twenty-five cents entrance.

Imagine the school, which made a fair-sized room with the desks cleared away, lit by hanging lamps. At one end a slightly raised platform, on which were arranged drinks and refreshments of various kinds, and all round the hall, the floor of which was not quite up to ball-room standard, benches were arranged. On the platform sat a single fiddler, a fine-looking young half-breed. The womenkind were all arrayed in their "joy-rags," and all the belles of the district were there. Most of the men had on their Sunday clothes, though some were not so respectably, but far more picturesquely, attired in dark trousers, light shirts, and bright-coloured scarves. All wore the inevitable Stetson hat, which always gives a Western impression to any get-up.

There were a great many half-breed men and girls, and their sallow features were quite as noticeable as the ruddy complexions of the English-speaking people. Somebody calls out, "Take your partners for the square dance."

The men rather shyly approach the girls and ask for the honour, which is readily given. Soon all is arranged, the fiddler strikes up a merry tune,

"MOLLY" AT THE WATER-HOLE ON THE LAKE

THE SETTLER'S BEST HELP

WHITAKER CUTTING ICE ON LAC LA NONNE
(Forty-two inches thick)

and one man stands on the platform and "calls out" the dance. A good "caller" is a very popular person at a dance. He does not simply call out each figure, but he keeps up a continuous stream of oratory in a sing-song voice, and apparently making some rhythm. At times his voice rises to a shout, which is quite necessary, as a great part of any square dance seems to consist in a kind of grand chain, in which the men stamp on the floor with their feet, keeping time with the fiddler. It was a curious scene. The little school filled with dancers, the single fiddler forming the only orchestra, and the caller—in this case a half-breed—shouting out the dance at the far end of the room.

Then came an interesting item—the Red River Jig. It is a difficult thing to dance well, and on this occasion was performed as a kind of exhibition by two half-breeds, a man and a girl, while the rest of us sat round and watched. The man was tall and handsome, the girl a typical half-breed, with sallow complexion and Indian features, dressed entirely in white. The jig was a most elaborate concern, which carried the man up and down the room, his feet going like blazes all the while, keeping time with the fiddle. The woman followed him, her feet going so fast that you could hardly see they were moving at all, and yet she did not go into any contortions like the man, but kept her body absolutely rigid. In fact you would almost have thought she was standing still on tiptoe, had you not seen her body just vibrating, like a top at full spin. Such an excellent performance of a dance, which few can now do well, was greeted with tremendous applause. The half-breeds are indefatigable dancers, and would go on till they almost drop with fatigue. The dance began about nine o'clock, and was not over till 6 A.M., when the last of the people left in their wagons or on horseback, with perhaps a ten or fifteen mile drive before them, with the temperature below zero.

Another very popular form of entertainment is the Box Social. The girls have prepared the boxes, which are decked out in ribbons. Each one contains a dainty "lunch" of sandwiches, cake, and pie. The boxes are put up for auction, and the young men buy them in, amid huge excitement. Of course the authorship of each box is supposed to be an absolute secret, but it soon leaks out who has made this with the blue ribbons, or that with the purple bows.

It is a glorious evening, and the schoolhouse is crowded. The auctioneer stands on the daïs.

"Gentlemen!" he shouts, as he holds up to view a dainty little box caparisoned in pink. "Gentlemen, I have here a box worth five dollars. What's the bidding?"

"One dollar and fifty cents," from a lanky Canadian youth in the corner.

"Say now, gentlemen, did you all hear that? One dollar and fifty cents. That fellow in the corner is a wise guy, that's a cinch! but he won't get a five-dollar box for one dollar and fifty cents. Now, gentlemen, any more bids?"

"Two dollars," laconically from a Scotchman. He must want a wife pretty badly. Eight shillings for a shilling's worth of food! But then the buyer has the right to eat his purchase with its maker, and there's a particular girl over in that corner—a Yorkshire lass—blushing to the roots of her hair.

"Two dollars, now that's a bit better! But, gentlemen, just look at this box!"

"Say now, I guess I'll go two dollars and fifty cents," says a young American who has been raised in Oklahoma.

"Three dollars," from the Scotchman.

The crowd twigged: $3—$3.50—$4—$5—$7—$9, it raced up, but the Scotchman, as always, was out to win. The box fell to him at ten dollars and fifty cents; and had you seen him, later in the evening, discussing its contents with the Yorkshire lass, you would have agreed that, though an expensive meal, it was well worth £2, 2*s*.

When the boxes have been disposed of, and incidentally a large amount of money gathered in for the school, or whatever good cause the proceeds are going to, a concert follows, and the evening almost always ends with the inevitable dance.

These are examples of the way in which the farmers and their families can, and often do, come together both in summer and winter. There is a strong Farmers' Association in this district, with which Dallas has identified himself. They hold frequent meetings, and have an Annual Agricultural Show every summer, when prizes are given to encourage every department of farming.

The long winters give time for reading. Though books are not very much in evidence, there is one publication which is always to be seen—Eaton's Catalogue; and the Book of Books would certainly have a wide effect on the life of the West, if it was studied with half as much care as the stock-in-trade of this great Winnipeg and Toronto Emporium. Nobody gets up very early. I have found some homesteaders learning various subjects through correspondence companies. One man was going through a course of Real Estate with a view to going into town and eventually starting on his own. As a matter of fact, this fellow had formerly been a business man in the States. Like so many others, he was an *amateur* farmer.

In the districts I am familiar with, there are comparatively few Britishers who have been *brought up* as farmers all their lives. Here is a list of the former occupations of some of our

English settlers, taken within a fairly small radius of this place:—Cobbler, carpenter, confectioner, groom, sailor, commercial traveller, soldier, plumber, traveller in the false-hair line, actor, tram conductor, railway porter, engine-driver, barber. Some of them—for instance, the cobbler, carpenter, plumber, or barber—can resort to their former trade for half the year, and thus make sufficient money to keep themselves and their families on their homestead the other six months.

What one cannot help noticing is that in the North-West to-day there are far too many homestead speculators—men who have no intention of making their homestead their home. Many are quite ready to admit that their one object is to "prove up" as soon as possible, and then clear out. It is true that till this country is well served with railways there is little opportunity for a man to make any money by staying on his farm, and I suppose speculating homesteaders are better than no settlers at all. But it is a serious thing when a settlement gets depopulated, and the traveller passes one empty shack after another. We have suffered somewhat severely in this way at Lac la Nonne.

It has often struck me as a little hard that the homestead conditions should be as severe for the British as they are for the American family. Britishers, from the very fact that they have come a long distance at a great expense to themselves, are at any rate not likely to sell their farm and leave the country altogether; while the Americans who have only to cross the border and come a comparatively short distance, take up land in Canada, "prove up," and then perhaps return to their old home, and hold their Canadian property as a good investment.

You have asked me several times whether the people are loyal to the Crown. It is a very difficult question to answer. In the first place, the West is receiving so many thousands of settlers every year, drawn from America, Eastern Canada, the British Isles, and every European country, great and small, that it is quite impossible at this stage to speak of "the people" as a corporate whole. One sentiment is noticeable with the majority of this cosmopolitan collection, after they have been living a few years in the country, and that is loyalty to Canada. Whether it is also accompanied by loyalty to the Empire depends on the country from which the particular family or individual sprang. There is a very strong feeling of Canadian nationality, which is growing every year; and among the British element, which is considerable, it is generally combined with attachment to the Empire.

Britishers who have been embittered by the hard conditions of their former life in the old country are sometimes rather contemptuous of the land of their birth. They have left for good and all an old society to which they feel no particular debt of gratitude, and they have made a new start in a new country where they are already beginning to prosper. Why should they concern themselves with the problems which, in their opinion, are the inevitable accompaniments of an effete civilisation? Canada is geographically too favourably placed, and as yet too young a country, to feel the real pinch of international politics.

On the other hand, those who at home took an interest in outside affairs and kept their horizon broad, are not blind to the advantage of sane imperial connections, though they would be just as strong as the others in their allegiance to Canadian nationalism. Indeed many of the more intelligent settlers, both British and Canadian, seem to feel that, though the papers often try to make out that Canadian nationalism is opposed to the imperial idea, yet the two things are really not in the least incompatible one with the other.

In Edmonton, and I think in most of the large cities, there are numbers of societies which exist for the purpose of bringing together those who hail from the same part of the British Isles, and of keeping strong the bond between the land of birth and the land of adoption. Such, for instance, as St. George's Society, St. Patrick's, St. David's, Sons of England, Caledonians, Sons of Yorkshire, Sons of Devon, and any number more of the same kind.

The national sentiment is being constantly fostered in newspaper articles and reviews, viz. "Sister states of the Empire, not daughter states." Henceforth, "Call us not children, but partners, whose partnership deeds can be cancelled by the junior partner to them." The very first Canadian newspaper I ever had in my hand, brought on board by a boy at Quebec, had a leading article on The Spirit of Canada, the whole point of which was the throwing off of a somewhat deprecatory colonialism and the development of a national consciousness.

In the older farming communities I am told that a large number of American settlers become naturalised, and therefore Canadianised, though, from what one can hear, it is not so much the case in the towns. The foreign element—German, Scandinavian, Italian, Austrian, Galician—are naturally concerned with their own interests more than with any outside questions, and are not in the least appealed to by anything in the shape of imperial sentiment. Indeed, they do not seem to take much interest even in local politics except when they are paid for their vote. They become naturalised after three years' residence in the country, and have a right to vote, thereafter presumably looking upon Canada as their home. The Britisher who settles in Alberta has a vote after a year's residence in the province and three months in a particular constituency,

The Canadian who only moves from Ontario to Alberta does not enjoy more favourable terms than these.

Sometimes among the more uneducated people there is a certain amount of ill-feeling. It is the custom among Americans to celebrate July 4th with a "picnic"—*i.e.* a social gathering generally consisting of sports and games followed by supper and a dance. No offence is meant or taken at this. Indeed the whole neighbourhood, irrespective of nationality, generally attends. Not long ago, such a gathering was held on July 4th near here. An American woman foolishly ran up the Stars and Stripes over the booth where meals were being served. Whereupon there was a great uproar, and the Canadian and English boys shouted it must come down. And it did; or else there would have been a free fight.

Personally, I think the action of these well-meaning patriots was a little mistaken. True, it was extraordinarily bad taste on the part of the American woman, as well as being outside the law, to run the flag up. But to the Americans, July 4th is just a holiday and nothing more. Many of those who make the day a cause for festivity are, to a large extent, ignorant of its historical significance. July 4th and no festivity would be like Christmas and no feast. Besides, even if it were done in a spirit of pride at what had been achieved on that day, there is such a thing as national courtesy. After all, July 4th is celebrated with full honours in London, and, as somebody said the other day in a review which I happened to see here—"Which is the more inspiring figure of the two—an Englishman sincerely and unreservedly honouring Washington, or an American raking among the dust-heap of the Revolution for his Anglophobiac fuel?"

However, it is only among the more poorly educated Americans, English or Canadians that there ever arises any feeling of this kind. As I said before, in the rural districts, many Americans become naturalised—indeed it is practically compulsory, as they cannot get their patents and become owners of their homestead till they have taken the oath of allegiance. And even if the parents never cease to look upon the States as their true home, their children will be Canadians.

Of course Canada has now for some time realised that she can pick and choose her immigrants. The qualifications necessary for the incoming settlers have been made more stringent during recent years, and I should imagine that when the great transcontinental railways are built they will tend to become still more severe.

I really do believe the old idea of sending "ne'er-do-weels" to the Colonies is very nearly exploded. It is a mere platitude to say that the prospective settler for the North-West needs not a smaller, but a more generous share of those qualities which are required to make a man successful in any country under any conditions. And what is true of the laity is equally true of the clergy. Only the other day a dignitary of the Canadian Church told me he had received a letter from a parish in England, asking if he could find work for a clergyman who "would do splendidly for the Colonies in every way; he only has one fault—he drinks a little too much occasionally!"

It is difficult to give you any idea of the kindness and hospitality of the people. Canada has been called "The Land of Open Doors," and out here, in the North-West at any rate, she certainly lives up to her reputation. It may be said that in a primitive state of society, where hotels are unknown, hospitality is not so much a virtue as a necessity, but to think or say this would be a gross injustice to the Western people. They are most wonderfully open-hearted and generous, especially to anyone travelling for the missionary cause. This does not alter the fact that every one is out to make every cent he can. I have not written much about the materialistic atmosphere of the country, which to be understood must have been *felt*, and to be *fully* understood must have been lived in for a considerable time. Letters from Canada are always full of this side of Western life. But when a man dedicates every particle of brain in his head and every muscle in his frame to the all-absorbing passion of dying a rich man—when he sacrifices every interest in life, and throws even the most sacred scruple to the winds in the craze for an ever larger balance at the bank—you can understand that religion (if it stands in the way) must necessarily, like everything else, go to the wall.

What strikes me as a layman so much is that a man is accepted almost entirely on his own merits. The non-Church people (and, åfter all, they are a considerable percentage of the whole) do not seem to understand or care whether one is ordained or not. They dump as a "preacher" priest and layworker alike. The missionary who goes to live and work in the West is thrown into a tremendously stimulating atmosphere, and he stands or falls by the kind of man he is, and the kind of work he does. The "preacher," from his very calling, is given a peculiar position in his district, but he has to justify it, and I can assure you, for a layman, it is a fearful responsibility.

I can't say I have a high opinion of Western courtesy. I say *Western*, not *Canadian*, purposely. The average Westerner's manners are primitive. Whether it is due to the infusion of Western American blood it would be hard to say. In the literary supplement you sent me out the other day, I read a review of a book called *The American People* by Maurice Low, in which the reviewer says: "The bad and scrambling manners of the

American people as a whole are clearly of the American's own making, traceable, as Mr. Low points out, first to the rebellion in revolutionary times against all things 'aristocratic,' and the desire of the more ignorant to assert their own 'equality,' and later, fostered by the rough circumstances of frontier life and the prevalent convictions among Americans of all classes that courtesy is only a waste of time in a world where the only thing that counts is getting there."

This may be true of the American—I don't know—but it is certainly true of the Westerner, who is a product of many cosmopolitan influences. His motto seems to be, "I am in this world simply to get out of it all I can for myself." Generally the Englishman soon gets used to the lower standard of manners, and it ceases to strike him as anything odd. But to the newcomer it seems as if the railroad official, the street car conductor, the man behind the counter, the ordinary person on the street, were all in a conspiracy to make him, the greenhorn, understand he is now in a country where class distinctions never existed and everyone is socially as good as his neighbour. It is very admirable and invigorating, yet there can be no doubt that this rather false sense of equality and independence is often made the excuse for great rudeness and a lack of the common urbanities of life. Of course the *educated* classes are in no way different from those of any other country. But it is the average uneducated Westerner, no matter from what part of the world he may hail, who, for fear apparently of being thought subservient, is often apt to lose sight of the fact that courtesy should prevail among equals. Britishers are often the worst offenders. To many of them, life in the West means a social step up. I remember, some months ago now, a cultured Canadian in Winnipeg telling me how intolerable some of the street car officials, who had come from England to that city, were. I suppose a little *tête montée* in their new surroundings.

I hope you will not mistake my meaning. I do not wish to make sweeping generalisations and lead you to think that *all* Westerners are rude and brusque. That, of course, would be ridiculous. There are many people, who, though they have roughed it in many lands, still retain all the old charm of manner which one always associates with a gentleman in whatever station of life he may be. Do not imagine either that I regret the death of class distinction. On the contrary, in my opinion, it is exactly this which is one of the most stimulating features of life in this great country. What one does resent are the unpleasant qualities which often seem to go with it.

Unfortunately it affects the children, who generally think themselves just as good as, if not better than, their parents. A Canadian boy is taught to "rustle" from the time he leaves his cradle, and he becomes extremely self-assured, self-reliant, and independent. Independence and self-assurance are excellent in themselves, but may easily become unhealthy if pushed to extremes; and, from all one can see for oneself and hear from others, there seems danger of this in the West of to-day.

There is one text in the Bible which most Western children seem to have inverted with admirable success from "Children, obey your parents" to "Parents, obey your children." They loathe the word "sorry." To bring a Western boy to a condition in which he is ready to make an apology is indeed a triumph. They have not very much idea of chivalry or sportsmanship, and are not renowned for saying "thank you."

Do not think that I blame them. Their manners are largely due to the poor upbringing they get at home, and the poor upbringing at home is chiefly due to that indefinable thing, the Spirit of the West.

They are 'cute enough—'cute as a Cockney lad. Ask a paper boy on the streets of Edmonton the way to some building. Without a second's hesitation comes the correct answer: "Two blocks west, one block south—buy a paper?" He has got hold of the maxim "nowt for nowt."

I should not call the average child well educated, but about all manner of things with which one would only expect a man to be familiar, he is extraordinarily *well informed.*

There is a magnificent system of education in Alberta. Here at Lac la Nonne there is a good country school, with an average attendance of about twenty children, British, American, Canadian, French-Canadian, half-breed, Scandinavian, and German.

In every township, with its 36 sections (each section being a square mile and containing four homesteads), numbers 11 and 29 cannot be taken in the ordinary way by settlers. When the district is developed, and the land goes up in value, these two sections, which are called school sections, are sold, and the proceeds go to the Education Department.

The Government give the settlement considerable financial help in running its school, and yet not enough to stifle local effort. When there are sufficient children, the settlers form a school district; say the district they incorporate consists of ten sections—*i.e.* ten square miles—that means between thirty and forty homesteads if the country is well settled, in a new country generally not nearly so many. The owners of these homesteads elect three of their number as school trustees, and the school tax is assessed at so many cents an acre—the maximum is 10 cents an acre. Absentee landlords, in the shape perhaps of companies who are holding up farm land, have to pay,

THE HEAD OF THE MISSION (*standing*) INSPECTING A NEW HORSE

MERCER (*on left*) STARTING FOR HIS DISTRICT AFTER A REUNION

otherwise their land can be sold. If the homesteader has arrears of taxes against him he cannot get his patent, even though he has fulfilled the other conditions. The school is then built in the centre of the district, and the local taxes are supplemented by a grant from the Government, which is based first on the size of the school district, secondly on the building and its equipment, the teaching, and the children's progress, and thirdly on the average attendance. It is very simple, and on the whole it works splendidly. A great difficulty is the lack of teachers, which has made it very tempting to admit American teachers on easy terms. But there is much to be said against a large influx of American teachers, who probably are ignorant of, and naturally indifferent to, Canadian institutions and English history.

An English teacher on entering Alberta is given a permit to teach for a certain time; then, if he wishes to take up teaching permanently, he must take a course at a normal school. Religious teaching can be given, if the trustees raise no objection, from 3.30 to 4.0 on Friday afternoons. We are sometimes able to avail ourselves of this opportunity. In one school near here I always teach on Friday afternoons, when I can get round, which means only once a month. A good Sunday-school, however, is the most satisfactory plan, though with regard to this there are, in a pioneer country, a great many obstacles, such as the difficulty of grading a small number of children, the different denominations of the parents, the distance some children always have to travel even to reach the most central point, the impassable trails in summer, the extreme cold in winter, the scarcity of qualified teachers, and, above all, the infrequent visits of the clergyman, which a huge district makes unavoidable.

We have got two horses here now—Bob and Paddy. At present I am using them as my team, but they are proving rather unmanageable. It is quite impossible for one man to hitch them up. Bob, who is not used to running double, generally waits till everything is done except to fasten the tugs (traces), and then, preliminary to bolting, stands for a few seconds upright on his hind legs and may come down in any direction—the betting is, with his feet over the pole. He nearly killed me the other day, and the team bolted with Whitaker yesterday, depositing the pole, the double trees, the rest of the sleigh, and him, at various points along the trail.

A GREAT CITY

THE MISSION HOUSE, EDMONTON,
ALBERTA, *March 28th.*

WHITAKER and I reached Edmonton yesterday for the Quarterly Reunion. You know the excellent system by which we all meet together in Edmonton whenever there is a fifth Sunday in the month. The fifth Sunday comes, roughly speaking, every three months, and as most of our country services are arranged on a monthly or fortnightly basis, this occasional fifth Sunday can quite conveniently be kept clear of engagements.

We found a good number of the men already arrived. The Mission now numbers twenty-two men, of which over half are clergy. The permanent staff at our headquarters here consists of Mr. Boyd (who is Head of the Mission and also Rector of St. Faith's Parish); Bailey, who has charge of a church in North Edmonton, a district which is rapidly growing and will probably in time become an industrial centre; and Blood, who has charge of a church at Calder, a suburb which takes in the Grand Trunk Pacific Railway yards, and will shortly be a part of Edmonton proper. The other three permanently here are laymen: Ault, Mr. Boyd's secretary; Cookie, whose name describes his work; and Carter, who is boss of the horses, cow, and garden. The rest of us are either on some country mission or along the Grand Trunk Pacific between here and the mountains. It would be difficult to exaggerate to you the value of these times of meeting.

The Reunion generally starts on a Thursday morning, and continues exactly a week. It is a rule of the Mission that every member of the brotherhood (however indispensable he may feel his presence in his own district to be!) must attend the whole of the Reunion, from the first till the last day. One day of the week is always set apart for Retreat. This generally begins with Evensong on the Thursday evening, and ends after the Celebration on Saturday morning.

Here is a typical day during the Reunion:

7 0	Morning Prayer
7 30	Holy Communion
8 15	Breakfast
8 45— 9 30	Chores (*i.e.* household work, stables or any odd job)
9 30—10 0	Meditation
10 0—11 0	Bible Study
11 0—12 45	General Meeting
12 45	Intercession
1 0	Dinner
6 0	Supper
7 0	Evensong
10 15	Cocoa
10 30	Compline

The prayer meeting which we have on the Friday evening of the "Quiet Day" gives opportunity to the whole body to pray for the wants of each individual member. In order to get a certain amount of continuity between the subjects to be prayed for, the intercessions are divided into three heads:

(1) Prayer for the world at large.
(2) Prayer for particular districts in the Mission.
(3) Prayer for individuals.

Meals are simple. Breakfast: porridge, bread and butter and tea. Dinner: meat, vegetables and pudding. Supper: eggs, or anything left from dinner, bread and butter, jam, cake, and tea.

The chore list we find posted on arrival. To some fall the washing-up or sweeping, to others bed-making, slop-emptying, or grooming. The list is put up by an elected Chore Committee. There is no appeal! I have been unfortunate this time, and have had a good deal of washing-up. Bed-making is a "snap" (*i.e.* a soft job), as there are no sheets but flannelette blankets.

It is quite delightful seeing everybody and hearing of prospects and problems in other parts of the Mission, and we have many long talks in the Library, which is the pleasantest room in the house, because it is the only one with an open fireplace. The General Meeting on the first day, when everyone gives an account of the work going on in his district, is one of the chief features of the Reunion. To-night I had supper with Sister Mary and Miss Warden at the Ladies' Mission House, which stands about fifty yards from our house on Mission property.

The number of people who, in the course of a week, stay at the Mission House, either for a meal or a bed, is remarkable. Take those who came yesterday as a sample. First, an attractive young Englishman, who wanted to know about land north-west. He stayed the night. Secondly, two fellows who came to ask if they could camp in our pasture. I suppose they have got jobs in Edmonton, and want to "bach" in a tent during the summer. Thirdly, two new members of the Mission arrived from England. Fourthly, a parson from Vegreville, a town south-east of here, for the day. Fifthly, a homesteader from Paddle River; he stayed the night, and the Mission could return some of the hospitality he had given our men up country. Lastly, two young fellows, strong Churchmen, who were going up into the Peace River country on a survey. They stayed to supper, and asked if Ault would forward their letters to them. This is besides all the usual parochial coming and going; for you must remember that the Mission House is also the centre of a thriving parish.

Edmonton is an unending source of interest, and it is always enjoyable going down into the city. Walk down Jasper Avenue, or any of the more important streets of the town, on any day you like, and you will be struck by the number of men who are standing about on the side walk or at the door of their offices in eager little groups, conversing about real estate or discussing the details of the latest big business "deal." There is an air about the Western business man which is quite foreign to the average "bread-winner" in London. The Westerner takes life very seriously. He wears an intense look on his face, which is seldom relaxed at any time during business hours, and he argues with vehemence in a somewhat nasal voice. He gives one the impression of being engaged on a great dollar-making campaign —a campaign which is lifelong, knowing no peace, not even a truce. Real estate and business matters are his one topic of conversation. There may be other interests hidden away behind a commercial exterior, but if this is so they are remarkably well concealed. He buys his evening paper to see the real estate market, takes it home with him, and discusses it over his supper with his wife, who has also had a flutter in land, and is as interested as her husband in these matters.

The Londoner has at least a safety-valve in sport. The evening paper is snapped up as much for the day's cricket as for the latest quotations. True, the average Westerner follows baseball with considerable interest, but no one could call sport one of the great interests of his life to the same extent as it is of the average Englishman's, or still more of the Australian's.

Then, again, there is always something new. I remember once asking a drummer (commercial traveller) in Calgary whether there was anything interesting to see there. "Not unless you were here three months ago," was the answer!

The Edmonton city motto is "Industry, Energy, and Enterprise," and it certainly lives up to it. The way the place grows simply beggars description. The streets are beautifully laid out in bouley-vards (so pronounced). A boulevard is a street with six feet of grass and a row of trees on each side of the road between it and the paths. The city occupies a large area. Except in the main business thoroughfares in the centre of the town, almost every house stands in its own lot. The houses are generally constructed of wood, which gives opportunity for exciting varieties of architecture. The most interesting thing at the present moment is the building of the high-level bridge which spans the huge Saskatchewan valley, linking up one bank to the other. Most cities in the West measure their progress by the number of skyscrapers they possess. But I believe there is a bye-law here which limits the height of buildings to ten storeys; so in Edmonton we shall never shine in this respect.

I always enjoy going down town to do some shopping. There are so many quaint sights. Here, for instance, is a huge wagon piled high with stores, furniture, and farm machinery, pulled by a strong team of horses, with perhaps an extra team and foal behind; the wagon is driven by a typical-looking Western boy, with large hat and yellow buff shirt, who lazily cracks his whip over his horses' heads. They may, for all one knows, be off on a trip of many hundreds of miles up country. They certainly look curious as they go lumbering along the main street of Edmonton. On the other side of the road stands a smart motor or a well turned out rig. On the pavement, rough railway men, miners, and odd customers of every kind jostle well-dressed women and smart business men. It is just as much a curious mixture as the buildings. Imposing-looking banks, small wooden shacks, and virgin bush, one next to the other, are still to be seen on some of the main streets of this wonderful city.

On one occasion I saw three fellows ride into town who looked like cow-boys straight out of the typical Western novel, with sombrero hats, green, red or blue shirts, big knotted scarves, white sheepskin "shaps," Mexican saddles and ropes, and splendid horses.

But you must not think of Edmonton as a rough primitive place with cow-boys "shooting up the town," and so forth. I believe even now many people in Europe have a kind of feeling at the back of their minds that the Far West is a country of cow-boys and Indians and wild uncivilised life. For this very reason some Englishmen when they come out here seem to be wanting in good taste. They treat a Western city as a place where they can go about in any old clothes, and behave in a very different way from what they would even in the country at home.

Edmonton has a population of fifty-five thousand people, and possesses such magnificent natural advantages that it will, before long, be one of the most beautiful cities of the whole Empire. Situated on the main lines of the two new Transcontinental railways—the Grand Trunk Pacific and Canadian Northern—connected with the C.P.R. through a direct line from Calgary, and destined to be the future base of all railways now building into the great Peace River country, it is rapidly becoming a large railway centre. Edmonton strikes me as a pleasanter place to live in than most provincial towns in England. It is certainly every bit as civilised, with its broad asphalted streets, large churches, banks, shops, and excellent tram service. Most of the brick buildings are at present extremely ugly. We are told that the art and especially the architecture of a particular age is the expression of its ideals. I must say I think that even Western ideals should not be judged by Western architecture.

The Hudson Bay Company have a large departmental store on Jasper Avenue. The large plate-glass windows are not so romantic as the log walls of old Fort Edmonton which Father Lacombe knew so well. The Indians used to bring their furs once a year to this old trading post, which still stands overlooking the beautiful Saskatchewan valley, almost under the shadow of the new Parliament Buildings.

The mother church of Edmonton is All Saints'. Archdeacon Gray, the Rector, is an old-timer in these parts, and has long kept the standard flying against great odds. In his time Edmonton has grown from a small town into a great city, and with it the life of the Church has steadily progressed. There are now at least eight Anglican churches in Edmonton, and All Saints', having grown far too small for its congregation, is moving two blocks further west, and is to rebuild on a much larger scale. The new building will be erected with a view to its becoming before long a pro-cathedral. There is no doubt that the time is nearly ripe for a new diocese with this city as its centre. There are thirty clergy working in the Archdeaconry of Edmonton, of whom ten are supported by their people. It is amazing what work the Bishop of Calgary manages to get through, but things are going so fast it is no longer possible for him to cope with the situation.[1]

It seems clear that Edmonton has a great future before it, when you remember that it is the capital of a province, which, besides having a larger area of land fit for cultivation than any other province in Canada, possesses an immense area of first-class timber land, and a mineral wealth hardly as yet realised.

I am writing quite *à la* " Sunny Alberta " style, but really it would be difficult to exaggerate the possibilities of this province. Industry and commerce are only just beginning to grow. There are few factories in Edmonton at present, but, with plenty of lumber and coal, they will come. The land in Southern and Central Alberta is absolutely bound to go up in value. Those who know the West well say that Canadian farm lands have a producing ability every bit as great as those of the Central or Western States. Indeed, the reports of the crops make that point clear, and besides, if it were not so, why should American farmers be flocking over the border in such numbers?

[1] The first meeting of the Synod of the new diocese of Edmonton was held in November 1913 at Edmonton under the presidency of Dr. Pinkham, Bishop of Calgary. Dr. Pinkham recalled the interesting fact that he had been consecrated Bishop of Saskatchewan in 1887, and that in 1889 he had had the privilege of presiding over the first Synod of the diocese of Calgary.

On January 29, 1914, Archdeacon Gray, who has given so many years of his life to North-Western Alberta, was elected first Bishop of Edmonton.

If you talk to some of these American farmers, as I have often done, you soon discover that Canadian farm land is *now* selling for the price at which land, say in the Dakotas or Nebraska or Kansas, sold fifty years ago. This looks as if Canadian farm lands would be a pretty sound investment. But the truth is that so many people have been able to make fortunes in real estate in an incredibly short time, that the slower, but surer, methods of money-making by developing the natural resources of the country, have simply been overlooked in the mad land gamble.

On the subject of real estate there have really been some very interesting transactions here. Of course, for the one man who makes a fortune with a splash, there are probably nine who don't, and you never hear of *them*. But still much money has been made, and land values in Edmonton at the present time are ridiculously high. I saw in my *Weekly Times* the other day that a writer on this subject said that it is a curious tradition that the first class to be attracted by land investments are clergymen, the second doctors, and the third small tradesmen. I suppose he means clergy in England or Eastern Canada. I should imagine that the Anglican clergy of Alberta, at any rate, might be acquitted on this score!

Let me give you one example of the rise in prices—in this case comparatively normal for the

West. It refers to one of the corners of Jasper Avenue and First Street; there are few more central or important sites in the whole of Edmonton.

Somewhere in the 'Eighties the Hudson Bay Company persuaded a settler to take the lot and live on it; but the settler tired of it, and sold it for 50 dollars. During the rush to Klondyke he went off seeking gold, and after travelling round in many parts of the West returned, after about fifteen years, to find his fifty-dollar lot had sold for 100,000 dollars. Its history, shortly, was this In 1900 it sold for 1500 dollars. The purchaser sold it again for the same sum, and later rebought it at 1300 dollars. Four years later he sold it for 7500 dollars; shortly afterwards it changed hands twice again for 10,000 dollars, and then 12,000 dollars. The purchaser of 1900 then got hold of it again. The C.N.R. steel arrived in Edmonton in 1906, and the day the last rail was laid the property went for 24,000 dollars. It eventually got into the hands of a Vancouver real estate firm, who last year parted with part of it to a Bank at the above-mentioned sum.[1]

Not long ago the Hudson's Bay Reserve was put on the market. In 1905 a large portion of the Reserve was not even surveyed. The popu-

[1] The opposite corner is said to have been traded in the early 'Eighties for a groggy black mare, and was sold in the summer of 1913 for 500,000 dollars.

lation of the city was then approximately 8000. There were no street cars and no pavements. Few of the municipal improvements since installed had even been considered. Settlement extended only to the east and south of the Reserve: there was practically no occupied residential section beyond. Since that time the property has increased in value purely through unearned increment. The Company simply paid the necessary annual taxes. When it was known that some of it was to be sold, there was such a rush for the property that the Company decided that the would-be buyers should ballot for the privilege of securing the best lots, in other words for the privilege of being allowed to buy the land at the prices demanded by the Company. Certain corner lots were, of course, much better located than others. The man who drew ticket No. 1 was entitled to buy what were considered the four best lots in the Reserve. I forget how many thousands of dollars he was offered for his ticket. There was an enormous queue of people waiting patiently to go up and draw a ticket, and people sold their places for large sums of money, though to be before some other man in the line was no guarantee that you would draw a ticket and he would not.

At Lethbridge they had something of the same kind. Some land near into town was thrown open for homesteading, and people were so anxious to secure the opportunity of "filing on"[1] that they came prepared to camp on the spot for days. The authorities got over the difficulty by chalking a square for each man on the pavement, and then photographing him on it. Their identity was thus assured, and they could go away and come back at the right time to file without further inconvenience.

Equally remarkable examples of rise in values can be quoted both here and in all the growing cities of the West. Saskatoon has the reputation of being the place in which more money has been rapidly made in real estate than any city. It was only founded seven or eight years ago, and already bids fair to become one of the most attractive cities of the West. The histories of Moose Jaw, Medicine Hat, Calgary, Vancouver, Victoria, Prince Rupert, all possess many examples of romantic land transactions.

While money can be made so easily, it is hardly to be wondered at that people have become land mad. Certainly, one gets absolutely tired to death of real estate talk.

Of course there has been a great deal of fraud, though I am not quite certain all the fault has been on the side of the land companies out here.

[1] *i.e.* entering their name on the register at the land office as prospective owners of the homestead, which would only become legally their property after the necessary conditions had been fulfilled.

"CHORES"

THE LIBRARY, MISSION HOUSE, EDMONTON

THE MISSION HOUSE, EDMONTON

If people in England or Eastern Canada buy property which they have not seen except through an absolutely reliable firm, they are foolish. The *Toronto Saturday Night* has lately been making a veritable crusade against subdividing in the West, and certainly the over-subdivision in some towns is ridiculous. Only a few days ago a man, whose word I trust, told me that a real estate agent had tried to sell him property on a well-known avenue in an equally well-known Western city. He had a map which showed the City Hall, then a little gap, and then came the property he was trying to dispose of; and dispose of it he did to numbers of people, the first payment being ten dollars, and then so much every month.

My friend, who was surprised, said, "How far from City Hall is it?"

"Oh, not very far."

"No, but how far is the property from the centre of the city?"

"Really, I don't know the exact distance, but not far."

"Well," said my friend, exasperated, "I happen to know how far that property is from City Hall —fourteen and a half miles."

The agent was a little taken aback. "We are trying to build up a town out there," he said apologetically.

It is generally the small men who are "stung"

—that is, the people who pay one instalment and go on paying more every month.

What would probably strike the new arrival most in any Western city is the countless number of real estate offices. From their windows, by means of placards and posters, maps, photographs and models, land in any and every part of the city within a radius of five to ten miles round is howling out to be bought. Now or never! Buy! Buy! Buy! Snap in Sunalta! Try Beacon Heights! Make your money work! Get rich quick! See the advantages of Saskhome! Here follows a long list of reasons why Saskhome is superior to any other property in or around the city.

Do not think I intend to imply these subdivisions are frauds. Many of them are all they claim to be. But it is always wise to see property before buying.

There are many people who say in a general off-hand sort of manner that all real estate men are rogues. But, of course, it is a perfectly legitimate business, and people who are defrauded generally have themselves to thank as much as anyone. The newspapers devote columns and pages to real estate advertisements. If a slump comes, and this source of revenue falls off, some of them will be in a bad way. The newspapers do not strike one as very good out here. They are poorly informed and badly printed. The other day one of them spoke of the Triple Alliance as being between Germany, Italy, and Australia. But perhaps that was only a misprint!

Last night I spent the evening at the University. I always go there when I can, because I know some of the younger members of the teaching staff and a few of the professors. They always give us a very warm welcome, and I need hardly tell you how pleasant it is to find oneself in cultured surroundings after one's ordinary life out here. The University is for the whole province, and is going to be a very big affair. It has a glorious situation overlooking the river Saskatchewan and commanding a magnificent view of all the northern part of Edmonton. Every year the number of students goes up by leaps and bounds, and the University is hard put to it to find sufficient residential accommodation, as at present only the first part of what will eventually be an imposing group of buildings has been erected. In close connection with the University there is a residential college belonging to the Methodists and housing about a hundred and fifty men; for the Presbyterian students there is a smaller college at present occupying temporary quarters. We have no college of any kind, though I should have thought that the Church had something to contribute to the life of a great University.[1] Mr. Boyd knows a number of the

[1] *Cf.* page 250 for question of an Anglican College in connection with the University of Alberta.

professors and often he gets one of them to come over to the Mission House at Reunion times and give us a lecture on literature or history. On one occasion Dr. Dyde, head of the Presbyterian college at the University, gave us a most interesting lecture on Reunion.

I had dinner to-day with McCormick. He is, as you know, head of the Church Camp Mission, the Canadian branch of the Navvy Mission Society. He has a good number of men working in various parts of Canada, and one or two west of Edmonton in the railway construction camps. He feels, and I imagine quite rightly, that a large amount of the influence his missionaries exercise in the camps is lost when the men drift into towns.

What a great thing it would be if some large Institute could be started in Edmonton, where a man could get a cheap bed, a good meal, and a game of pool, without the fear of being "doped," and then fleeced. It is reckoned that some hundreds of men pass through Edmonton every week during the summer months. Any time one goes down town one can see scores of them at every street corner, or round the saloons and pool rooms. Some place, where they could leave their baggage, and to which they could have their letters sent, would in itself be of considerable value.

Round the employment bureaus there are

always crowds of men scanning the advertisement boards on which are chalked up all kinds of jobs:—

> WANTED.—20 teamsters for railroad construction work. West. 3 dollars a day. Ship to-night. Fare advanced.
>
> WANTED.—100 labourers for grade. North. Ship to-morrow morning. 2·75 a day. Fares advanced.
>
> WANTED.—First-class cook for large sawmill camp. North-East. 75 dollars a month.
>
> WANTED.—5 first-class carpenters for work near town. 75 cents an hour.

This morning I was standing in front of one of these bureaus scanning the boards when the agent came out and said:

"Say, young fellow, want to drive a team out West? Fare advanced and good wages."

I declined the offer.

"Don't want to leave town perhaps?" he persisted. "I could fix you up with a nice job, as grocer's assistant. How would that do?"

I declined this also, and I am afraid he put me down as a poor lot. His persuasiveness was quite intelligible, as the agents get a fee of one dollar for every man they place; for this reason some of them are rather lavish in their praise of various jobs, and hold out every inducement regardless of whether their statements are true or not.

During the season when the building rush is on, enormous wages are paid for skilled labour in Edmonton. Plasterers 90 cents an *hour—i.e.* 7.20 (28*s.*) a *day*. Carpenters 65–75 cents an hour. Work at this remuneration could be had in these trades for probably six months in the year. The other months are slack owing to the cold weather. There is also the higher cost of living: but even taking into consideration these two disadvantages, a comparison with European conditions will show that the skilled workman, if he keeps steady, has found an Eldorado in Western Canada.

There is some probability that I may be sent out West myself pretty soon, in which case I shall get closer knowledge of the problems which must necessarily arise from the gigantic work of building two great railways from coast to coast.

I had a game of football this evening. It is astonishing how soccer has taken out here. Of course it is largely "old country men" who play it. Baseball will always find hundreds of devotees in the West, where the American element is so strong. But perhaps you may remember that the Corinthians came out here some time ago. I came in to play for them, and though we did not have to exert ourselves over much and won very easily, yet the football was not at all bad, and there was a large crowd—and much enthusiasm at the game. But I don't think sport of any kind is too clean out here. There is too much of what is called "rooting" on the part of the crowd—that is, shouting objectionable remarks at the referee and questioning his decision at every point.

ALONG THE NEW TRANS-CONTINENTAL

THE MISSION HOUSE, EDSON,
ALBERTA, *June 20th.*

I WRITE to you from a new address. It is some time since you had a letter, and I want now, if I can, to give you some impression of the last two or three weeks.

I do not know whether you are familiar with the main points of railway geography in North-Western Alberta at the present time.[1] They are simple. The Grand Trunk Pacific and the Canadian Northern Railways (which I will refer to in future as the G.T.P. and C.N.R.) are both building as rapidly as they can towards the Pacific. They both passed Edmonton long ago, but the C.N.R., who arrived there first, only went twenty miles farther west to Stony Plain, where it stopped, and for the next few years every energy was put into developing the system farther east and south. The G.T.P., however, arriving in Edmonton a couple of years later, went straight on west, with the result that it is now farther ahead than the C.N.R. Both railways run

[1] *Cf.* map, p. 256.

ENTWISTLE CHURCH

THE REV. G. S. PROVIS, G. BOUSTEAD (*behind*), AND AUTHOR AT EDSON

THE TWO TRANSCONTINENTALS, G.T.P. AND C.N.R.
(Running within eighty yards of each other near Marlboro)

almost side by side from Edmonton up to and through the Rockies. Their route is determined by the Yellowhead Pass,[1] through which both have to go. The G.T.P. at the present moment is on the other side of the mountains some miles into British Columbia. The C.N.R. is still on the Yellowhead Pass. The boundary between British Columbia and Alberta runs down the summit of the mountains, so that on reaching the top of the Yellowhead Pass, you go from one province into the other.

At a particular point on the Western slope of the mountains, about fifty miles into British Columbia, the two railways part company. The G.T.P. goes a little north, and then west to Prince Rupert on the Pacific Coast; the C.N.R. runs south-west, over the Albreda Pass, and so to Vancouver.

This latter company are also building a branch into the Peace River country, which leaves the main line at Onoway and will run north-west right through the Greencourt country to Dunvegan. As yet, however, they have not begun to operate any trains for more than a few miles beyond Edmonton, so one reaches Edson and other points farther west over the G.T.P.

I started west from Edmonton just over two weeks ago. There is only one train west a day,

[1] The summit of the Yellowhead Pass is about 250 miles due west of Edmonton.

and it leaves Edmonton at 6.30 in the morning. It seemed quite curious being in a train again—the first time for over a year. The railway officials are somewhat stern, and when one looks at the type of man with whom they are constantly dealing, one can hardly blame them.

The station was a scene of great activity at that early hour of the morning. The long train, with its huge cow-catcher locomotive, was drawn up at the platform. Crowds of people, almost all *men*, some carrying "grips" (*i.e.* small suit-case or bag), others blankets or packs of various descriptions, were hurrying to find seats or pushing their way towards the booking-office or baggage-room. Vehicles of various descriptions were driving up to the station, laden with baggage, and it really was a marvel where everybody and everything was going.

The train reaches Edson at 1 P.M., a distance of about a hundred and forty miles, and returns the same evening. There were scores of foreigners and men of the rougher type, evidently going into the camps.

We went clanging out of the station well on time, the bell which is carried by every locomotive going "fit to beat the band." The train stopped at every station, but the first place of any size we came to was Stony Plain. We have a church and mission-house there, worked by Mercer from Onoway.

Another twenty miles took us to Wabamun. Here, too, we have a church and mission-house with Huxtable in charge. It is a beautiful place right on Wabamun Lake, which is fourteen miles long, and likely to become a very popular pleasure resort for the people of Edmonton. A further hour's run brought us to Entwistle, sixty miles west of Edmonton, called after one of the early settlers. It is a place which really originated at the time the G.T.P. were putting their bridge across the Pembina —the same river which I know so well at Wild Horse valley, Belvedere, and other points farther north; only here it is infinitely finer, as it runs through steep wooded banks two hundred feet high. Our little church and house stand only a short distance from the edge of the cliff, from where there is a magnificent view of the river which rushes and sparkles below, taking great sweeping bends to the north and south.

The population of the town is not very large, and varies a good deal. The C.N.R. are building a steel bridge over the Pembina very similar to that of the G.T.P., and they are also going to put a depot (*i.e.* station) just north of our church; so Entwistle will be well located as regards railways, as it will have a station on both the great Transcontinentals. It seems quite ridiculous that these two railways should run so close together in such a huge country as this, but, as I said before, it is the pass through the mountains which dictates the route. At present the G.T.P. station is a mile east of the town, but the people are petitioning to have it placed nearer.

The train stopped to dump down freight and a few passengers. The place looked very much like any other little Western town, with its two or three stores, post office, pool room, &c., all displaying a pretentious perpendicular front to the street, but behind of rather a less showy character.

After leaving Entwistle the country is wild. Sometimes we were passing through land heavily timbered with jack-pine and spruce; then again came huge stretches of muskeg, covered with young fir trees, which appear to thrive in this swampy soil. The grading must have been costly and laborious through this kind of country. A few miles farther, and the train is passing through a veritable forest of poles, bare tapering tree trunks gaunt and burnt, stretching up in every kind of fantastic shape, left in this condition by some great fire.

A succession of thick untrained bush, muskeg, hills, creeks, and lakes—that is a true description of this country. At any rate, not many signs of agriculture were to be seen. Round some of the stations, which are all built on the same pattern, and seem to recur about every seven or eight miles, whether there is any reason for them or not, centre a few houses and possibly a farm or two. At Junkins, for instance, there was a barn, a restaurant, a stopping-place, and a few shacks and tents. The forests and the muskegs are endless. In one way, it is the immensity of this country which cannot fail at once to impress and attract, and yet in some respects I cannot help feeling that the actual grandeur or beauty of a particular piece of scenery is somewhat spoilt by its constant repetition. Over and over again, one has a sense that there is a surfeit of everything and one longs for a little piece of real English rural landscape. Canadian scenery, instead of impressing, is sometimes apt to oppress. But it probably all depends upon what mood one is in!

Round Entwistle a good many bears have been seen. In fact, they are becoming more of a nuisance than a curiosity. The chance of seeing one up here is better than in more settled farming districts.

Nine miles short of Edson we crossed Wolf Creek and the McCleod River. The G.T.P. have two fine steel bridges over these waterways. We seemed fairly high, and had a magnificent view of great rolling hills and valleys entirely covered with rough timber.

At Wolf Creek there are a number of deserted houses and barns. It was for many months the head of steel, while these two bridges were being built. The head of steel is the point where, for the time being, the actual steel rails end. Here a kind of temporary town springs up. The people live in rough log shacks and tents, and keep stopping-places, barns, restaurants, and stores, which the presence of large numbers of freighters makes both necessary and lucrative. The trains bring up provisions, machinery, and all the other requirements for railway construction to this point, and they are then taken the rest of their journey in wagons, and deposited in the camps at various points. As much freighting as possible is done in the winter, because then large loads can be hauled over the trails, which perhaps are almost impassable in summer. The stores are then put in large "caches" (*i.e.* large tents or specially constructed log shelters) at convenient points along the right of way, and are ready for the arrival of the hosts of men in the spring.

Wolf Creek was head of steel for nearly a year—much longer than usual—because the two bridges took some time to construct. In its palmy days there was a town of many hundreds of people, and they built a school for the children. At one time there were a thousand teams freighting west from there. Now it is all empty and deserted; most of the shacks and barns are roofless, and the windows either removed or broken. The whole place, which has a pleasant position along the high river bank north of the track, looks solitary and depressing. There are a fair number of homesteaders in the district, and Provis goes over there to hold a service occasionally. But the little village is all gone, and the freighters have moved on further west.

Bickerdike, nine miles west of Edson, was the next head of steel, where there is a long trestle bridge and a branch line south-west, but now that also has sunk back into comparative unimportance, and the population has moved on still farther west.

At last came Edson. It is a place which has hardly made as rapid progress as its most enthusiastic supporters hoped, but has probably suffered more from its friends, who have over-boomed it, than from its enemies. I should think that the town has a considerable future before it. It will serve as the centre of a steadily growing farming community. And, more important than this, it is a divisional point of the G.T.P., which has already erected large workshops there. The C.N.R. main line goes through a place called Tollerton, only four miles south of Edson.

Edson is far the largest place west of Edmonton at present, and boasts some twelve hundred people, a Mayor, and a City Council. Main Street is built on a hill side, and gives a character to the place at once, and our church, with its bell tower, has a magnificent site right on this principal street, crowning the crest of the hill. If ever this town becomes a large place, and the time comes to erect a brick building, with a proper tower or steeple, the Anglican church will strike the eye directly one arrives in Edson.

The shack stands behind the church. It is one-storeyed, and consists of three rooms—a living room, a small study, and a bedroom containing several bunks arranged as on board ship. I got in by the back door, and found Provis[1] out. Having had no dinner, I ferreted about and discovered some bread and butter and cold ham, and then, over a pipe, read several numbers of *The Edson Leader* which I found lying about.

The local paper has only one *raison d'être*, and that is, to boost the town. Those who have speculated well but not wisely in town lots, only need to glance through the columns of the local journal to find the most invigorating cordial for their drooping spirits. Here, at any rate, there is no question about future prosperity. Boundless self-assurance and amazing confidence in its own future are the chief characteristics of every Western town. Turn over the pages of *The Edson Leader*, published weekly, owned, and

[1] The Rev. G. S. Provis, member of the Mission, and in charge of Edson and district, June 1911–July 1913.

EDSON, 1910
(Consisting of one stopping-place kept by a Chinaman)

EDSON, 1912

GRANDE PRAIRIE AND PEACE RIVER MAIL LEAVING EDSON

controlled by local men. Half of one page is thus occupied :—

DO		HELP TO
IT	WHAT?	BOOST
NOW!		EDSON

AND BUILD IT UP

What can I do? One thing you can do is to support the Paper instead of knocking it. The support of a community is as much needed to build up a good newspaper as it is to build up a good Store. Some people unfortunately are just as well satisfied to build up a Store or Paper a thousand miles away in which they have no interest, as one at home. Are you one of them?

On the first page there are two columns on the doings of the Grand Trunk Pacific Railway out West. The completion of the Transcontinental line intimately concerns the future of the town, and the allotment of so much space to this subject is only natural. Another column recounts the transactions of the weekly meeting of the Town Council. Part of the paper, which contains serial stories and anecdotes, and other small items of news, is supplied by a company in Eastern Canada. On page 4, there is a short leader entitled "Edson's Birthday," part of which is before me as I write this letter, and I will quote it, as it is a typical example of the remarkable growth of the West.

"Two years ago to-day the Edson Post Office was established at the back of a store. One sack once a week carried the mail. On the 1st October, 1910, the office was entrusted with money order business, but the mail still arrived once a week. Now, of course, Edson has a fully equipped post office, doing every sort of post-office business, savings bank, annuity, &c., and for the last week or two the total cash business done at this office has averaged $2000 per day—there is no mistake in the cyphers here—it is $2000 a day.

"That is not all. When that one sack used to poke itself into the town, it contained the mail not only for this place, but for the territory now served by the post offices at Bickerdike, Marlboro, Ernstead, Hinton, Pocahontas, and Fitzhugh. Now these offices get their mail direct, and, without that, a drayload of mail comes into the Edson office six times a week. From Edson, the mail to the North is carried by stage, leaving here twice a week, and includes mail addressed to Grande Prairie, Beaver Lodge, Saskatoon Lake, Spirit River, and Dunvegan, all in Alberta, and Fort St. John and Pouce Coupée in British Columbia. The last semi-weekly load for this despatch weighed seven hundred and one pounds."

This is surely wonderful progress for two years! At the top of a column on the same page are these words, "Boosting Edson is like making love to a widow—you can't overdo it." Fill up the rest of the paper with a number of local advertisements, and you have the whole thing. There is no general political news to speak of. The paper does not exist for that purpose, even if it could afford it. Its primary object is *advertisement*, and as a good many copies are sent away each week, it probably answers its purpose; at any rate it satisfies the *amour propre* of the people of Edson. No self-respecting town is without a journal of its own; it would be as much as its life was worth.

Provis got back to take the service next day, which was Sunday, and I helped in any way I could. Afterwards a number of fellows came round to the shack, and we smoked and had coffee. Talk mostly centred round the future of Edson, railway progress, and the possibilities of places like Fort George—always interesting conversation, I think.

Boustead,[1] who has been doing missionary work out here for the past year and a half, arrived on the one o'clock train on Monday, and, having talked over plans, we arranged to go further West the next day.

Accordingly, on Tuesday morning, he and I were down at the station by 7.30, and boarded a long freight train standing in the yards: the last

[1] Mr. Gerald Boustead, a layman, joined the Mission in the autumn of 1910.

car was a "caboose"—*i.e.* the car on which the train crew live. Every train out here has its train crew, which seems to consist of the conductor (*i.e.* guard), a couple of brakemen, and the train agent, who sells and collects tickets on the train. The caboose was fitted up with a chair and table for the freight agent, seats on two sides which act as bunks at night, a cook-stove, and two or three cupboards. There was a "cupola," which is a raised look-out place.

With a big jolt and much creaking, off we went, travelling slowly with a good many stops. At one place we passed "an extra gang," who are always on the move up and down the line ballasting up the track wherever it has sagged. The whole track, of course, is permanently patrolled by section gangs, working under a section boss, who is responsible for a stretch of about seven or eight miles, *i.e.* an equal distance on each side of a station. At every place we came to, out jumped the crew and dumped down the freight. These little stations have no station-master—agents or operators they are called out here—they look absolutely deserted, except for the family of the section boss, who generally live there. One cannot help wondering why there is a station at all, and still more why some of them have such curious names. If there is no local name or historical incident to suggest a title, stations often receive the name of some prominent official of the Company—such, for instance, are Bickerdike, Dandurand, Pedley, and Hinton; but whoever was responsible for perpetuating the name of Junkins was certainly misguided.

At one station I was leaning out over the rail at the end of the caboose, when a fellow on the track came up and said:

"Say, boy, got any chewing tobacco?"

"No."

"No tobacco at all?" he said, as he looked at my pipe.

"Yes, some smoking tobacco," I said, and handed him a bag of it.

He looked at it, took out about three pipefuls with his fingers, opened his mouth wide, and shoved it all in.

"That's great dope," he said with a broad grin, and was off.

At a station called Dandurand we got off the train, and walked along the track to Marlboro.

This settlement has been brought into being through the discovery of marl (hence the name Marlboro) and the consequent construction of cement works. Everyone in the place is directly connected with this work.

There is nothing here to remind you of the beautiful Wiltshire town. No broad picturesque street of ancient red-brick houses, but a straight row of hideous lumber buildings. The first is a store, the next a pool room, next to that again an hotel, then come a couple of bunkhouses, a large stable, and finally, on some rising ground, our shack and the church. Add a number of shacks of various size and shapes, scattered around through the bush, where a certain number of married families are living, and you have a fair idea of Marlboro, Alberta. At present it is more of a camp than a town, and in the bunk-houses live some hundred and fifty men employed on the work. They are of every nationality and class—Canadians, Americans, English, Scotch, and Irish, Poles, Russians, Germans, French, Swedes, and numbers of Galicians. Some are coarse and degraded; others have seen better days, and find life in a bunkhouse hard. Some spend their life going from one camp to another as labourers, others are homesteaders and farmers, and are here for a few months to make a "grub-stake."

Our shack cost sixty-five dollars, and is a "snap" (*i.e* a good bargain) at that. It is just a little lumber building of one room, though there is a partition separating off two bunks. That night the mosquitoes were fearful, and will, I suppose, become still more of a scourge, until they are killed by the early frosts which generally occur at the end of August. They seem to make a bee-line for any part of your body which is at all exposed, and lose no time in getting into action. But still there is one thing about the mosquitoes here—they generally give warning of their coming by a loud "Ping." In Alaska, I believe, they are intolerable, being comparatively small, quite silent, and far worse bloodsuckers.

The following day I caught the train which runs three times a week westward from Edson, intending if possible to get as far as Fitzhugh. There was some doubt whether I could do so, because my pass, which the Grand Trunk Pacific most kindly grant to the three of us who are doing missionary work up here, had not come, and ordinary passengers could not get beyond Hinton, sixty miles this side of Fitzhugh. The agent came along the train to sell tickets.

"Where to?" he asked.

"Fitzhugh."

"Where's your pass?"

"I haven't got one," I replied, and then explained it was probably then on the way from Winnipeg.

"Without a pass you can't get beyond Hinton."

This made me anxious. It was not a question of money. I was willing to pay full fare, of course, if only he would allow me to travel. The difficulty was that the line beyond Hinton was not open to passengers.

"Well," I said, "I may not look like it, but I'm a missionary, and I want particularly to get up there if I can."

"Guess I've heard that before," he said; "how can I tell you're not a spotter?"

A spotter is a man entrusted by the Company with the detestable job of travelling incognito over their lines to see if the officials are carrying out their work properly and are incorrupt.

"One of the brakemen who knows me can answer I'm not that," I said.

"Now don't get sore about it," he said; "I'll sell you a ticket to Hinton, and if you were to give me a five-spot[1] you wouldn't get any farther."

But as good luck would have it, I caught sight of an official at Hinton whom I had met only a few days before in Edson. I told him my plight.

"I guess I can fix that," he said, and spoke to the train agent, who even then seemed doubtful, but, more through sheer importunity, I think, than anything else, let me through.

Of course I paid my fare, and the agent, who was perfectly right in refusing to take me, was appeased a few days later when he saw my pass, which was forwarded from Edmonton.

Hinton is situated at the very entrance to the mountains. It looked a temporary kind of place, with its straggling row of saloons, restaurant, stores, barns, and shanties, all facing the station.

From here westwards the scenery is grand. The G.T.P. track skirts the southern bank of the

[1] A five-dollar bill.

APPROACHING THE YELLOWHEAD PASS

Athabasca, which turns and twists in a most bewildering fashion, its steep banks well covered with dark pines. Above, tower great jagged masses of rock, the higher slopes covered with snow. At one point we came out on the shores of a lake about a mile broad and several miles long. Straight from the opposite side rose the mountainous peaks, almost lost in the clouds. The surface of the water was like glass, in which every detail of rock, bush, stream and snow, was faithfully reflected. The peaks vary considerably in height and shape.

Now and then we passed some little encampment in the forests, but for the most part the country seemed wild and uninhabited. The G.T.P. construction camps were farther on than this, though remains of them were constantly to be seen in the shape of old disused shacks and barns, large clearings in the bush, tins, and other refuse.

After a time we reached Pocahontas, where there is a considerable settlement, owing to the development of large coal-mines by the Jasper Park Collieries, who are supplying the G.T.P. with sufficient coal for their western section.

On a small white board, attached to one of the telegraph poles opposite the little shanty serving as the Pocahontas Station, were the figures 1001, which meant the number of miles we then were west of Winnipeg.

The clouds seemed to have got very low, and by the time we steamed into Fitzhugh, with much clanging of the bell, it was pouring with rain.

Fitzhugh is situated in Jasper Park Reserve, a large tract of country reserved by the Government for the nation. No game may be shot in it, and, as the Government have not yet surveyed the town-site, Fitzhugh is little more than a camp. The place consists of the depot, the round-house (for engines), and railway yards, a large restaurant and hotel, a hospital, a store kept by the doctor, and a few houses dotted about here and there in the bush.

The valley is not more than three-quarters of a mile broad, and on each side the hills rise steeply, the lower slopes covered with pines, which seem to find some root in the rocky crags The mountains are not so much covered as heavily sprinkled with snow, and they take on every fantastic shape you can imagine. Fitzhugh is entirely surrounded by these immense castellated peaks. The country looked wild, unexplored, uninhabitable, and unkempt.

A curious assortment of men jumped from our train, and hurried up to Beecham's stopping-place to get accommodation for the night. Most of them were going on first thing next morning to the front. I stayed the night with most hospitable people called Hamilton. Mr. Hamilton is conductor on the train which runs every day from

Fitzhugh to the end of steel and back, and I arranged to accompany him on his trip the following day.

After supper I went round to see the doctor, who keeps the only store in the place. He is the G.T.P. doctor, and has many curious cases to attend. The other night he was sent for to see a Galician labourer in a car some way down the track. The man did not seem very bad, and the doctor asked him if he had been eating anything which disagreed with him. The Galician shook his head, but a friend (?) lying close to him volunteered the information that he had eaten twenty-seven sausages for breakfast. I can quite believe this. I myself have seen a man eat eleven boiled eggs straight off, and follow them up with meat, vegetables, and pudding.

The next morning I was down early to catch the train going west. To watch the crowd was an education in itself. If Canada can assimilate such a cosmopolitan collection as this, she will do well. Great fair-haired Swedes, sallow-faced Italians and Galicians, black swarthy-looking Russians, keen-featured Yankees and Canadians, and not a few strong-looking fellows "with the map of England written plain on their face." They wore all kinds of clothes and all kinds of headgear, and nearly every one carried a pack or a roll of blankets.

As the conductor backed his "mixed" train

(*i.e.* passenger and freight combined) into the station, there was a general stampede for the two passenger coaches which were at the end, behind a long row of flat gravel cars. I found a seat at the far end, among a whole bunch of foreigners, who talked continuously and seemed excited about nothing. They behave very much like animals, and when they get a little drink in them they are far worse than animals. While we waited they began to eat, passing round huge hunks of bread out of which they each took a bite in turn, and then some awful pink concoction in a bowl into which they each stuck a dirty fork, or possibly their still dirtier fingers.

Not far from me was an English-speaking fellow, who was wearing an attractive costume, being completely dressed in a moose-hide suit, with beautifully embroidered facings. Some of the men were already drunk. One fellow in front of me fell down as he was climbing up into the car, but his friends bundled him in somehow, and he kept reeling up and down the train, making himself a great nuisance. The cars were of the rough colonist type, and showed signs of hard usage, which is not surprising when one saw the type of men who used them.

Not long after we started, the conductor made his way down the train and beckoned me to follow him. I was taken into the baggage car, where I made the acquaintance of the train crew, namely the two brakemen, the train agent, and the newsagent. The main passenger trains in this country are provided with a newsagent, a loquacious individual who continually walks from one end of the train to the other selling papers, tobacco, and candies. Here I made the whole trip, sitting on a packing-case before the big folding doors, which gave one a fine opportunity of seeing the country.

As the train was a mixed passenger and freight, we were constantly stopping at various places to take on or put off "flat-cars" full of gravel, or "dump-cars" full of "dirt" deposited there by the steam shovel, trucks loaded with rails or ties, "box-cars" full of provisions, coal or lumber—all the hundred and one things which were wanted up at the front by the camps.

Letters and packages were shovelled off in the most bewildering way at various points along the line. One of the brakemen would lean out as we passed some gang of men, and heave a big parcel into the middle of them.

On one occasion, having stopped alongside a dilapidated train, the moving home of a large gang of labourers, we were already starting again when the brakeman suddenly ejaculated, "Gee whiz, those two cases should have been put out here." "Quick, then," says the conductor; "dump 'em out right now." The two cases are seized, pushed through the wide doors, and fall with a crunching kind of thud on the grade below.

Somebody puts his head out of the stationary train, and says in a very sarcastic voice, "With care, I guess, eh?" and sure enough, as the cases roll over, there, in big letters, are scrawled "With Care." But the train had taken us well out of hearing.

The valley now began to narrow down, and as we went puffing along above the Athabasca, here only an infant river, the scene was indescribably beautiful. Not much grading had been done as far as this on the C.N.R., and when one saw the work at that stage it gave one a good idea of what engineering skill and human labour can perform, in converting a mere survey line into a level track which will carry a train over deep gullies, through rock cuts, and along the banks of mountain torrents.

The G.T.P. and C.N.R. certainly possess a remarkable gradient. The rise was hardly noticeable. We had a heavy train and only one engine. For a train climbing the eastern slope of the mountains the grade is only four-tenths of one per cent., and only for about twenty miles is the gradient higher than this for a train coming up from the West.

About seventeen miles from Fitzhugh, we reached the summit of the Yellowhead Pass. Here there is a station also called Yellowhead; it is merely a collection of log shanties, near which stands a little obelisk, about five feet in height, on one side of which is written *Alberta*, on the other *British Columbia*. The name Yellowhead is supposed to have arisen from an Indian trapper, who, travelling up and down over the pass, traded with Jasper Hawes, the representative in this lonely district of the Hudson's Bay Company. The trapper rejoiced in light reddish-coloured hair, and therefore received the nickname of Tête Jaune from the Indians. Hence the name of the pass, subsequently translated into Yellowhead.

The valley was very narrow and the heavy timber successfully hid from view anything which might be considered the source of the Athabasca. But Yellowhead was hardly left behind, before one caught sight of the Fraser River wending its way through the forests towards the Pacific. On the British Columbia side of the pass the country opens out, and the Fraser, after flowing into Yellowhead Lake and then into Moose Lake, reappears as a river of respectable size.

At the west end of Moose lake is Mile 28—the farthest point to which the train runs. For the convenience of engineers and contractors, various points along the newly-constructed line are designated by their mileage from a particular place. The mileage starts at one, and runs up perhaps as far as Mile 150—often higher if need be. But, generally, about every 120 or 130 miles a new division begins. For instance, a new division was started at Wolf Creek, and runs right away up to the summit of the pass. Here the boundary between Alberta and British Columbia was made the opportunity for starting again at Mile 1, and the point we had now reached was called, in railway parlance, Mile 28, B.C.—28 miles into British Columbia from the summit of the Yellowhead. As soon as possible stations are built, and as a matter of fact Mile 28 will soon rejoice in the name of Resplendent.

Here, on the banks of the Fraser, has grown up a regular little settlement. It consists of a number of shacks and tents, but, like all head of steel towns, its day will soon be over, and it will have to give place to Mile 53, which is Tête Jaune Cache. Up to now, Mile 28 has been the base from which all freighting has been done.

You must bear in mind that the Railway Company does not undertake its own construction work. It is all let out to contractors, and Foley, Welsh & Stewart are the great contractors in the West. A powerful company like this takes on perhaps a good many hundred miles of grading. But they sublet practically every yard of it to smaller companies, who in turn may sublet again. In any case, the work itself is performed by armies of hired labourers, who are paid so much a day. Foley, Welsh & Stewart contract with the G.T.P. to do the whole work for so much, and, in the same way, sub-contractors agree with

WINTER GARB

SKY-PILOT ON THE FRASER

"SKY-PILOT" ON THE "HIKE"
(Having shot his dinner)

A SECTION GANG

Foley, Welsh & Stewart to build a certain distance for a certain sum. The estimate is made on the amount of "dirt" to be removed from one place to another. The rate per cubic yard varies, of course, with the nature of the soil. Rock work naturally commands the highest price, loose rock and shale the next, and ordinary "dirt," *i.e.* soil or clay, the lowest. Quite often, if the work proves more difficult than had been expected, the estimate is found to be too low, and the contractor therefore loses heavily.

The smallest contract is that taken by the "station" man. Station work is let out in stretches of 100 feet. It is mostly pick and shovel and wheelbarrow work (in comparison to more difficult grading, where steam shovels and heavy graders are necessary). Several men generally take on station work together. They are their own masters, and, as long as they have the work properly done by a certain time, can do it when and how they like. They make "big money," but work fearfully hard.

The men, none of whom had been allowed to get as far as Mile 28 without possessing a Foley, Welsh & Stewart certificate, headed in big letters CONTRACT TO WORK, tumbled out of the train, and were told to walk some little distance to a stopping-place, from where they would be forwarded next day to their various destinations.

I had dinner with the train crew and a number of other men at Foley, Welsh & Stewart's camp at Mile 28. The food was good, but roughly served, and I confess to surreptitiously rubbing my knife and fork on my overalls before using them.

We started back to Fitzhugh about 3 P.M., carrying with us quite a number of men who were leaving the camps. I gathered that there was a good deal of ill-feeling between the contractors and the men. There is probably fault on both sides. The contractors don't treat the men any too well, and the men often treat the contractors badly.

The other day seventy-five men, each of whom had had his fare (amounting to 22 dollars apiece) advanced from Winnipeg to his destination, were taken up to the head of steel. Of course the fare had been advanced on the sole understanding that they would work in the camps. Next morning, when the train went up again, the seventy-five men were all waiting to be taken back. The contractor's agent came to the conductor of the train and said, "You see those seventy-five men there? They each of them owe the Company 22 dollars—they've refused to work, and I guess you'd better not take them back on your train."

The conductor thought the men had not got much of a case, so did as he was asked. The engineer was instructed to back the train about a quarter of a mile out of the station. All the proper passengers were carefully taken up, and the train passed the seventy-five men at about thirty miles an hour. Such language, shaking of fists, and deadly threats had seldom been seen or heard before. If looks could have killed that train crew, they would have been dead men on the spot. Next day when they came up, they passed the men in twos and threes straggling back to Fitzhugh.

If fellows don't like a job, they just quit right away, regardless of contract or anything else; or perhaps a man may think he would like to see something of this country, and have a free ride into the bargain. He goes to the agent in Edmonton, Calgary, Winnipeg, wherever it may be; gets his fare advanced, which implies that at least he will stay long enough in camp to work it off; and then "jumps the job" long before he gets there. A man can be prosecuted for this, and sometimes is, if he is caught. The contractors stand to lose a good deal of money by this kind of thing, and perhaps are somewhat apt to take it out of the men when they get a chance.

We got back to Fitzhugh that night, and the next day or two I visited in and around Fitzhugh. On Sunday afternoon we had a service in Mr. Hamilton's house, at which quite a number were present, amongst others, the Methodist student who has been living in Fitzhugh for a time, and will shortly be returning to college.

I should have left next morning, had not the doctor asked me to stay and take the funeral of a Russian patient, who, he said, could not live many hours. The man had been sent down from Mile 28 with double pneumonia, and I had already seen him once or twice when visiting in the hospital.

By law the G.T.P. have to supply doctors and hospital accommodation for the men, and at Fitzhugh there is a small lumber hospital holding eight or nine beds. On Saturday I had been in specially to see a young Englishman whose hand had been fearfully crushed. He was driving an engine out West which was hauling away the dump cars, after they had been filled with dirt by the steam shovel. The shovel had come to rock, and a small charge of dynamite had been put in. He did not know this, or at anyrate did not understand, as the labourers were all Galicians. A huge piece of a tree trunk, becoming dislodged by the charge, struck his right hand against the cab of the engine and reduced it to a pulp. Thus a fellow in the prime of life, earning 150 dollars a month, and intending to make a home for his sister, was struck down in a second. He will never have the use of his right arm again.

The other patients consisted of a Canadian, another Englishman, a Bulgarian, an Austrian, a Frenchman, a Spaniard, and the Russian of whom the doctor spoke.

Nobody understood Russian, and he knew not a single word of any other language. I went over on Sunday and Monday to see him. He made signs for a pencil, but was really too weak to write. We could only discover that he came from Bessarabia, and the doctor was not certain that we ever had his name right; so how can his parents be communicated with? He lay there hour after hour on the point of death. As he was evidently a member of the Greek Catholic Church, we cut him out a cross of blue paper, at which he gazed enraptured. During the afternoon we got a swarthy Russian, who had just come into Fitzhugh and could talk a little English, to come and see him. It was a curious scene—the little wooden room which served as a ward; the other beds occupied by this cosmopolitan crew wide-eyed in their curiosity; the sick man lying there gasping, his eyes so glassy and face so pallid that one would have thought him dead, had not one heard the quick uncertain breath; the doctor, myself, and a Galician boy standing round; and on his knees by the bedside, his lips quite near to the sick man's ear, the great black-bearded Russian. He did what he could, but it was of no avail. The man was too far gone to speak.

About 5 P.M. I returned to the hospital, and

found the bed screened off with blankets, roughly rigged up with ropes. From the other side came dreadful sounds. I went in at once, and found Williams, the orderly, holding the poor man down by his arms, while another man was holding his legs. It was the most horrible death scene that I have ever witnessed. The man was absolutely yellow in colour, and was choking and fighting for breath. This fearful fight went on for nearly half an hour. The wooden hospital was very close, and behind the blankets it was almost unbearable. Two or three of the foreigners were peeping round to see the last. One would never have believed that a man in his condition could have had the strength to fight for so long. Then suddenly, with a gurgle, he seemed to give it up, and sank back dead. I said the Commendatory Prayer, or as much of it as I could remember, as he passed away, and then we tied up his head and wrapped him in a blanket. The doctor had already ordered a rough wooden box from one of the men at the station, and, by the time he was washed and ready, they brought it over to the hospital. He was put into it, nailed down, and put outside; there was nowhere else to put him.

Next day, after seeing the park ranger about the burial place, the doctor and I went down with four labourers on a hand-car to a place where there is a flat stretch of land near the Athabasca River. Here, where an Indian baby

TYPICAL RAILWAY CONSTRUCTION CAMP

LAYING STEEL OVER A TRESTLE BRIDGE

THE RUSSIAN'S GRAVE

and a Finlander were already buried, we told the men to dig the grave for the Russian. A more beautiful place no one could desire for a last resting-place. Imagine a long stretch of short green grass, sloping down to the Athabasca, and all round young green pines; opposite, the hills rose steeply from the river, and away to the east shone the snow-covered peak of Mount Hardisty. Behind us, the forest-covered slopes ran right up to the rocky cliffs of Pyramid Mountain, and along the side of the hill went the great Transcontinental line, in the construction of which this man, like many another, had met his death.

The doctor and I went back and got a wagon, on which we placed the coffin. I jumped up with the driver, who had much difficulty in restraining his language, because his team of grey mules was obstreperous; but the gravity of the situation made him do his level best, and it really was humorous to see a sudden outburst hastily smothered with a furtive look at me. Williams rode with us, and sat on the coffin, the only place there was. Our curious funeral procession went bumping along over a vile trail, and when at last we reached the place we found the grave ready and the men sitting round smoking.

"Say, parson, we've dug it good and deep," said the foreman; "he won't be popping up again next spring as some of 'em do!"

We lowered the coffin into the grave at once,

and then I put on cassock, surplice, and hood, and read the Burial Service. The men stood round with bare heads, and one of them threw earth on the coffin at the right moment. After the service was over, they did not take long to shovel back the sandy soil. Another fellow and I cut down some small spruce trees, put posts and rails round the grave, and made a cross. We wrote the date on the cross, but not his name, as we did not know it for certain. So there we left him, and another is added to the number of those who never return. It is a tragedy which is enacted over and over again out here. Pioneer work demands its toll; and nowhere a heavier one than in railway construction.

Yesterday afternoon I got back here.

LUMBER CAMPS

MARLBORO (140 miles west of Edmonton on the Grand Trunk Pacific main line),
ALBERTA, *October 9th.*

I FORGET whether you have a clear idea what this place, Marlboro, consists of or not. There are a hundred and fifty men employed in installing the cement plant. A few of these are married, and have their own shacks; others are banded together in groups of two or three, and have built themselves little shacks or loghouses—this is rather the more permanent element, they feed in the cookhouse, but sleep and spend the evening in their own shacks; and lastly, there are three or four bunkhouses, where the bulk of the men sleep and spend practically all their time when not at work. The bunkhouse men are of all nationalities, and the foreign element generally keeps together. Two of the bunkhouses are predominantly English-speaking.

When I am here I spend almost every evening in the camp. Take last night as an instance. After supper, which I had in my own shack, consisting of fried eggs, bread and marmalade, and tea, two or three of the men came up to help me finish the inside of the church. It is curious that one of my chief helpers has been a strong Roman Catholic. After an hour I went out, with some of the latest Edmonton and Winnipeg papers under my arm, bound for one of the English-speaking bunkhouses. It had been sleeting and snowing a horrible wet snow all day, so the whole camp was inches deep in slush, mud, and standing water—it was cold and very damp.

Imagine a long low building of lumber, covered with black tar paper; it looks dingy enough. The door when opened lets out an atmosphere reeking with coal oil, bad tobacco, and wet socks. On the right are two tiers of wooden bunks, each tier consisting of two bunks side by side. The men are pretty closely packed. A bench runs along by the bunks, and this, with several boxes and tree stumps, forms the sitting accommodation. The floor is covered with mud and slush, brought in by many pairs of boots—the said boots, with the socks which belong to them, are hung up in various advantageous positions near the central heater in which a huge wood fire is roaring.

The men themselves, in various forms of *deshabillé*, are sitting and sprawling about on the benches, smoking and talking; while some are so tired with the day's work that they are already rolled up in their blankets and snoring. Round the stove they are all English-speaking, but at the far end there are three or four Italians jabbering away, and, just on my left, as I enter, are some swarthy-looking fellows who look like Spaniards. At any rate they are Dagos, which is a convenient term, and includes any dark-visaged individuals, such as Spaniards, Italians, or Galicians. As I live in the place, I knew a good many of the men, and, after distributing the papers, I stayed and had a long chat. The other night (a Sunday) we had a service in this bunk-house. The men sang so long, I thought they would never stop, while the accompaniment was a concertina and two mouth organs, the latter played by two Baptists with more noise than discretion.

Generally speaking, the average man in a camp seems to have two great topics of conversation—whisky and women. There are some men who have spent a good part of their lives in bunkhouses, and, when the day's work is over, it is a difficult job to attract them out into any higher or more civilising atmosphere They are generally shy, and often ignorant and prejudiced. One can only hope to make a beginning by going into the bunkhouses, taking them good literature, getting to know them and helping them individually. Often the work seems slow, and there is little visible result.

The greatest curse of this country is undoubtedly drink. *By law* no alcoholic drink is allowed in or near a construction camp of any description, but "boose" gets in occasionally, and then fellows will get drunk before mid-day. In many cases it is fearfully pathetic. Men fly to the wilds to escape drink, but even there unscrupulous people pursue them with it.

Often for two or three weeks there is not a sign of whisky in the place. Then, all of a sudden, some "bootlegger," as the man who brings in the drink is called, sneaks into camp with a bagful, or a bunch of men come up from Edmonton with their pockets bulging, and the whole camp seems to go mad. It seems as if this class of man *has* to drink, and too often the authorities wink at it. All the boss wants to do is to keep his men, and if he thinks he can handle them better by shutting his eyes to the drink—or even by facilitating its arrival—he probably will do so. Morals don't enter into the question at all, and often it is not only drink but worse forms of vice which are tolerated and even provided. In this camp, however, the authorities have done all they possibly can to keep bad influences out.

The havoc which whisky works when you get it into a construction camp is hard to describe. Here in this camp, for instance, is the cook, an Englishman from Liverpool eight years ago—a man who is a real master of his art, and has been earning 100 to 125 dollars (£20 to £25) a month, plus board and lodging, ever since he came to this country. On Saturday night he was in my shack, and over a desultory game of draughts we touched on the drink question. He was sensible enough too, and told me he could have saved thousands of dollars by investing them profitably in real estate, had it not been for alcohol. Yet, yesterday and to-day, he has been half-crazy with whisky—the meals have all been at sixes and sevens, and a bunch of 70 or 80 men kept waiting for their dinner, although they have only half an hour at noon. This is a most unpardonable offence in their eyes, and they were ready to pull down the cook-shack over his ears.

Very often it is the hard drinkers who are the best workers, and for this reason a man who neither drinks, smokes, nor swears is apt to be considered soft and not much good. It almost looks as if the very fact that they are a rowdy bunch who go on the drunk, makes them in their sober intervals first-rate men at their job. To create any public opinion on the drink question seems totally impossible. Excess in drink is looked upon as a necessary evil, or, it would be more true to say, a necessary pleasure. Some drink openly—some secretly—while some try to keep off it out here, but talk perfectly frankly about going "on the drunk" when they reach Edmonton.

There are a number of steel-workers here, all men who have been making good wages for years, and yet they have not saved a cent. It has all gone in gambling or drink. The worst of it is that they play into the hands of sharks in the towns, who are out for nothing else but to rob men coming in from the camps with money in their pockets. A fellow whom I know well told me he had a drink at a respectable hotel in Edmonton. He is not a man who drinks too much, and on this occasion he had just one glass of port. Almost immediately he fell down in a torpor, and lost consciousness. When he woke up three and a half hours later, his pockets had been turned out, but fortunately he had practically no money with him.

If this kind of thing is done once, it is done scores of times every day in the big towns. The sharks take care to drink little or nothing themselves, and too often the bar-tender is in league with them. I could tell you of man after man who has been "doped" and "rolled"—in other words, drugged and robbed. It is impossible to persuade the men of the folly of going into a saloon with their pockets full of money. They would run almost any risk to get a drink. They are extraordinarily happy-go-lucky. One day you may find a fellow working in some camp out West, and a few months later you may run up against him in Edmonton looking affluent and well-groomed. One year he will be working his way across the Atlantic in a cattle-boat, the next, travelling first-class. Money is easily earned and as easily spent.

The only thing to do is to get to know as many men as possible, and to study them. Then it may be possible to help individuals, but really I often feel a man might not be here at all for the impression he seems to make. It is so fearfully difficult sometimes to know when to speak and what to speak. Even to suggest that a place like this is *crying out* for the ministrations of the Church is a gross perversion of the facts. But, after all, that only makes the *need* for our work all the greater. With a bunch of men like this, all the usual standards of morality are thrown to the winds. I do not mean to say that the men are a lot of devils—on the contrary, they are extremely generous and open-hearted and wonderfully good to me—but when they get away from the restraints and conventionalities of civilisation, all their principles seem to disappear, and their notions of right and wrong become dangerously unbalanced.

However, there are many encouragements, so I suppose I ought not to feel depressed. For instance, when I was visiting a bachelor the other night in his shack, he produced some money for the Church, saying, in a most delightful way, that as long as he was in the camp and as long as I was there, I was to count on the same amount from him every month. This man was a Presbyterian.

Then, again, besides the bunkhouse services,

there has been a steadily growing number of men at our Sunday afternoon service in church. The church used to be at Bickerdike (in other words, Mile 22) when that was the head of steel and there were 1000 people there. Now there is not one person left. So Boustead took the church down, put it on a box-car, and erected it here. Head of steel, as you know, is now right away in British Columbia, the other side of the mountains.

We have a regular Church Service in the afternoon, using a slightly shortened form of Evensong, and really there has been a splendid number every time. The congregation is an extraordinarily mixed one, comprising every kind of denomination, but there is not the least doubt that when people get to understand our service, and become familiar with its arrangement and meaning, they appreciate its quiet order and dignified language. There are always some who do not like a set form of service, but it is curious to see how several of the denominations out here seem to be gradually moving towards something of the same kind.

Quite a number of men come up to my shack at night to see the papers and write letters, and to-morrow night my reading-roomshould be ready. The company have put up a lumber building with double floors and walls, so that, in spite of a canvas roof, it will be warm. The Reading Camp Association are for the present supplying

CHURCH AND SHACK, MARLBORO

LAYING STEEL A MILE A DAY IN THE MOUNTAINS
(Notice ties being forwarded on the further side and rails on this side. See p. 215)

us with all sorts of daily papers and periodicals. I have got some really comfortable canvas chairs, and bought writing-paper and pens so that the men can write their letters, while the Company have supplied games. From what the men have said, I feel confident that, through the winter months at any rate, it will be largely used. We shall have foreign papers, as there are so many non-English-speaking men, especially Galicians, in the camp.

The latter are difficult people to make much of. Cooks always say they are the most ungrateful and captious men to feed. A pancake slightly over-cooked, a potato discoloured, the meat a trifle tough, and they "kick"—*i.e.* make a row about it. They consume far more meat than English-speaking men, and expect to get an enormous amount of it. A cook at Edson told me each man eats on an average 2½ pounds of beef a day. They get from 2.50 to 3 dollars per day in wages, whereas in their native country they probably worked from morning to night for a mere pittance, and had the simplest of food.

One finds numbers of Galicians on the section gangs—platelayers we should call them—who keep the permanent way in repair. The section boss here has two such men who have been with him nearly two years. They only make twenty cents an hour, but it is a "straight 20 cents"—that is, they earn their money all the year round, whatever the weather. They board themselves very cheaply, and seldom "blow their money in," their idea being to save a few thousand dollars and then go back to their native country, where such a sum will enable them to live in luxury for the rest of their lives.

There are a good number of men working here who have been out West in the construction camps, and most of them are very strong in their condemnation of the contractors for the way in which they treat their employees. It is very difficult to get at the true state of affairs, and from what I have seen I should say there was fault on both sides. Certainly twelve dollars for a pair of boots, five to ten dollars for a pair of blankets, forty cents for a twenty-five cent packet of tobacco, and twenty-five cents for a ten cent cake of soap do seem excessively high prices. On the other hand, the contractors have to freight everything into the camps at great expense, and are often treated dishonourably by the men.

They are constantly having inquiries. Not long ago, at the instance of the Italian Consulate, the Department of Labour took the matter up. The report said that, on the whole, the men were fairly treated. Labourers often complained of excessive cost of transportation—*i.e.* from Edmonton to the camps. What the contractors do is to deduct the railway fare from the wages, but if a man remains for more than six months this is refunded to him.

I think it is a real grievance that the men are paid by cheques. When they start out for civilisation they have no money, and are forced to ask the train agent or some other individual to cash their time cheque at a discount of ten per cent. But it is very difficult to say what the contractors can do otherwise. They cannot keep enough money in hand to pay every man in currency.

Last week I went off to visit several lumber camps in this neighbourhood. With my pack full of literature, I started on foot westwards, along the G.T.P. track. It was a brilliantly sunny afternoon, frosty and yet warm. The line runs along the steep northern bank of the McCleod; on the other side, the low undulating hills are heavily timbered, and stretch right to the foot of the mountains, behind which, as the short afternoon drew to a close, the sun set in a perfect glory of red and gold. In winter, when the atmosphere makes distances extremely clear, the whole of this district is dominated by the jagged range of snow-covered peaks.

I was beginning to wonder how much farther it was, when I saw cheerful lights shining through the trees, and five minutes brought me into a splendidly built logging camp—a large cookhouse, a still larger bunkhouse, barns, and offices

—all lumber, which is cheaper than logs when, as was the case here, the camp was run in connection with a mill.

The cook received me most hospitably, and asked me to have supper with him and the cookee, the men having had theirs. I gladly accepted the offer, having had nothing since 12 o'clock. There were between 50 and 60 men in camp, and only one bunkhouse, so that was obviously the place in which to hold the service.

It is always a critical moment when one enters a bunkhouse full of men for the first time. Generally what happens is that the men just glance at the newcomer, size him up, and then pay no more heed to him. This indifference is almost harder to cope with than hostility—it is really more unpleasant to be ignored than jeered at. The missionary has got to "get busy," and do something. The best way is to have a good stock of reading matter with one, and in a logging camp, miles away in the bush, magazines and papers are always a godsend. To begin giving these round is a splendid introduction.

This particular bunkhouse was the biggest and cleanest I have ever yet seen—it had only been built a couple of weeks. I opened the door and walked in. There must have been over fifty men in it—some were lying in their bunks or sitting on the benches which ran down the middle of the room. On my left were a group of men gathered round a grindstone putting a good edge on their axes; to the right were a group of French Canadians talking and laughing with many gesticulations; round a table in the middle were gathered a number of men gambling; and at the far end a square dance was in full swing. Two fiddlers were playing a jig, beating time with their feet, another fellow was calling the dance at the top of his voice, and a number of huge lumberjacks were hopping around like so many ballet-girls. They were an extraordinarily nice set of fellows, and, as soon as they realised who I was, stopped the dancing in the middle of the set.

"Say, Parson, you hold your meeting right now, and we'll get on with the jig when you're through."

"Sure I will, and I guess you can play a few hymn tunes as well as jigs?" I said, turning to the two fiddlers.

They laughed uneasily, shyly, like school-girls. Great big men they were, dressed in crimson shirts open at the throat, and yellow corduroy trousers. One was the best axeman in the camp, and, as I was told afterwards, came from Glengarry.

"Oh! I guess so, Parson, if we know 'em."

We fixed on a few with which they were familiar. I asked the gamblers to stop for half an hour, and they consented with perfect courtesy, sweeping the money and the cards off the table.

I stood in the middle under rather a poor oil lamp, and had to speak loud to make myself heard. They sang sitting, but I got them all to stand for the General Confession, which I said alone very slowly, explaining first exactly what we were going to do.

I can tell you it was a fine sight to see all those great men standing in absolute silence while I said the familiar words. We had plenty of singing, and I read from the Bible and gave an absolutely simple talk. After it was over, the dancers fell to with renewed vigour, and I stayed chatting to those who were sitting round watching.

One man who had only just come up from Eastern Canada shook me warmly by the hand afterwards, and said he hadn't expected Christianity would have spread that far West. Another fellow came up, and addressed me like this:—

"Say, Parson, what Church do you belong to?"

"To the Anglican Church."

"That's good." And he went off to his bunk, returning in a few moments with two small books by Walsham How.

"Now," he said, "I've read these, and I want to be confirmed. My home's down in Saskatchewan, but I won't be down there yet awhile, as I've got a job in Edmonton for some months. You can give me the name of a parson in Edmonton if you like, and I guess I'll go and see him when I get down there."

Cases like this make the work seem worth while.

Among others, I got talking to a curious old man, grey-haired and rather battered. He had been in Minnesota and Wisconsin at the time of the last Indian massacre, when many white people were scalped. Some of his stories were too awful for words. He remembered going into one house where the whole family had evidently been surprised by the Indians in the middle of their mid-day meal. The husband and wife lay scalped on the floor, and the children were sitting round the table alive, but with a nail through the hands of each one, pinning them to the table.

Next day I tramped on about fifteen miles, and reached my destination, another lumber camp, about 2 P.M. As this was long after the dinner hour, I felt doubtful about getting anything to eat. On going into camp one of the most important people to see is the cook. Cooks are proverbially cantankerous. If everything is not just O.K. (all correct), or if (as they think) they are unduly interfered with, out they go without a moment's warning, however awkward it may be for the boss. If the cook is a good one and satisfies the men—and it is remarkable to what extent the men consult "little Mary" as to whether they shall stay or quit—you can be sure that the boss of the camp will be scared to death lest the cook should be rubbed up the wrong way. Sometimes, as one boss put it to me, cookology and theology don't go very well together. Friendly with the cook, and half the battle's won.

Often the best place for the service is the cookhouse, which, needless to say, is under the direct government of the cook. Inside this building he is a veritable autocrat, and as long as he gives them good food the men obey him implicitly, and will go to some lengths to be in his good books. If the cook is unwilling to help the preacher, there are many excuses which can be quite legitimately urged against the use of the cookhouse. In the camps a considerable amount of food is left on the table all day, in the shape of butter, biscuits, cake, and stewed fruits. These are often covered with thin gauze to protect them from the host of flies which in summer infest such places. For a service, the tables must be completely cleared, otherwise the men begin picking and eating. This means trouble for the cookees (the cook's assistants), and the cook can easily say his cookees won't stand the extra work.

As a matter of fact, one often has reason to be just as grateful to these hard-working, good-natured "hash-slingers," ever ready with chaff and quick repartee, as to their autocratic boss.

Still the cook, though cranky and requiring

careful handling, nearly always turns out to be a real good sort, and it is quite the exception if he does not invite the preacher to come in to any meal he likes, as well as give him permission to put up a notice in the cookhouse where every man in the camp will see it.

Such a man was Bill, the cook at this particular lumber camp. He is an old-timer, as old-timers in the West go. When the Grand Trunk Pacific was no farther than Wolf Creek, three or four years ago, Bill used to keep a stopping-place at Mile 22—that is 22 miles beyond the end of steel, on Foley's trail—and enjoyed the reputation of putting up a better meal than anyone else on the road, when pork and beans were the only items on the menu.

I made for the cook-shack, and had hardly crossed the threshold before a small clean-shaven bullet-headed man, with his cook's cap cocked on the back of his head, launched himself towards me, and a hand was thrust out in greeting.

"Hello, Parson, how's yourself? Glad to see you. How did I know you was the parson? Why, Gor bli' me, I know a parson when I sees one, with his pack on his back. Had dinner? No? Well, I guess you're just in time to sit in with the cook; and how's McCormick?"

And hardly giving me time to answer, he rattled on.

"Mac, why he was a fine boy, Mac was!

'Bill,' he used to say, 'Bill, you're an old sinner, but your heart's in the right place.' Why, I kept him at my place a week once, and it never cost him a cent. No, sir, there's never a preacher yet who's paid Bill a nickel. The boy had come down from 65, and his moccasins, why they was pretty well worn through—it was kind of cold then too, thirty degrees below or more, and his feet was that sore and frostbitten that I says to him, 'Now, Mac,' I says, 'you quit hiking for a bit, and don't you hit that trail no more till I get your feet fixed up.' My! you fellows, you have a hard time of it. Well, well—I guess we've all had hard times in this country. I tell you, Parson, right now, this West ain't a country for a fellow to be down and out in. It's a darned fine country, you bet your life it is, for anyone as knows how to get a move on and look after himself, but if not, why he'd better get right out. 'Beat it,' I says to them sort—'beat it, you'll never do no good in this country.'"

"You're well fixed, Bill?"

"Well, Parson, I tell you, when I opened my stopping-place I had one dollar and twenty cents in my pocket. Me and another fellow we bought out a tie-camp outfit[1]—you're eating off one of the tin plates right now—and when we'd got the log-shack up and everything fixed, well, believe

[1] *i.e.* a camp of men occupied in felling trees and shaping them into ties (sleepers).

me, we hadn't got much left. But Pat Burns' outfit they was good to me, and Ben who kept the store, he let me have my stuff on credit—and I paid 'em back, every cent, at the end of the month. But I was telling you—my partner he comes in one day and says, 'Bill,' he says, 'we'd best get out of here afore we starve. The Grand Trunk don't figure on getting busy till next spring, and there'll be nothing doing.'

"'Jack,' says I, 'there's never man yet who said *you're beat* to old Bill, and there ain't going to be neither, that's a cinch. I ain't got a cent anyways,' I says, 'to make Edmonton with. If you've got cold feet,' I says, 'I guess you can quit right now, but here I stays.' Well I stuck right there, and I worked hard, Parson—worked night and day from October to March—we had packers[1] through, and there was a right of way bunch staying with me for quite a time. 'Boys,' I says to 'em, 'I'll board you alright a dollar a day—pork and beans and a bit of fish, and I can promise you good bread, and that's all.' Well, I got through, and made good too. Jack he came back after a bit, and brought some stuff out with him—some flour, tinned goods, and a case of whisky. I take a snort[2] now and again, Parson—any harm, eh?"

I told him I thought he was a fool to drink.

[1] *i.e.* men in charge of a train of pack ponies freighting stuff to the front on trails impossible for wagons.

[2] One of the numerous Western expressions for a drink.

" But I don't hang out a shingle as being a saint, Parson. Still I'm not such a reprobate as you might think. Guess I *may* have some wings somewheres, if only you could see 'em."

" I guess you'll get 'em burnt off one day."

Bill looked at me sharply, and then grinned.

" Well, Parson, p'raps you're not far wrong neither. Guess I'm in the line up for hell all right—with no return ticket either. But a fellow must have a blow-in sometimes, you know, and a bottle of boose does make a man feel good." And he got up from the table as if the last remark had finished the argument.

" I guess you'll be wanting the cook-shack for a meeting to-night, eh? Well, you can have it at 7.30, but don't you figure on me being there. I was raised a Catholic, and I ain't seen the inside of a church these fifteen years, and I wouldn't go now anyways. I can play the fiddle a bit, though," he added with some pride; "and I'll play the company a few airs if you like, when you're through with your preaching. I guess you'll be getting along into the bunkhouses now for a bit to see the men, eh? Round 'em up, Parson, round 'em up. It'll do 'em good to have a meeting; and let me tell you one thing—a fellow on your job don't want to be too holy in this Western country, but I guess you'll be all right."

It took me a long time to decide whether this could be considered a compliment or not.

MAIN STREET, TÊTE JAUNE CACHE, JANUARY 1913

We had a good service that night; the boys turned out well. True to his promise, Bill didn't come, though I could see his shadow, head on one side, arms akimbo, listening intently, through the curtain which separated the kitchen from the rest of the room, and afterward he sallied jauntily forth, and played the Intermezzo from *Cavalleria Rusticana* exceedingly well on his violin.

I got back to a station on the main line shortly before midnight, and caught the train to Marlboro. It is a curious experience stopping and boarding a train at this time of the night. The section boss and his men had all retired to bed, and the little wooden station was deserted. A stable lantern had been left burning in the waiting-room. Directly the roar of the engine is heard in the distance, the intending passenger goes out into the middle of the track and swings the lantern backwards and forwards to "flag" the train. Then, having blown out the lantern, and left it where he found it, he clambers up on to the train, which only pulls up for a few seconds.

Coming down from the West, the train is generally full of men leaving the construction camps, and to climb straight out of the clear frosty atmosphere into one of the cars, in which the men are closely packed, is like entering some stinking cockpit. The cars are generally rather over-heated, and the men are mostly lying on the berths which let down from each side. The walk down the narrow gangway frŏm end to end of the car is a distinct strain on the nasal organs. But it is certainly an interesting sight to see all these great burly men of every nationality, each one, no doubt, with a substantial cheque in his pocket, which he means to cash and then "blow-in" the money. What a harvest for the saloon-keepers of Edmonton is this nightly arrival of men!

The building of these two great Transcontinentals has meant a lot to Edmonton, when one remembers that all the provisions for this army of men comes from or passes through that city, and practically every dollar of the colossal annual pay-roll is cashed there.

I came down in the train with the Inspector of the R.N.W.M.P. for this division — a delightful man and a first-class officer. We talked a good deal about a murder which had taken place some time ago at Mile 29, B.C., when a fellow called Taft had shot dead a huge giant of a man, the largest labourer on the grade out West. It was over a game of cards, but the quarrel was a long-standing one.

British Columbia is, of course, outside the jurisdiction of the Mounted Police, who are only responsible for the country districts of Manitoba, Saskatchewan, and Alberta. Considering that we have a good many rough characters out here, it is marvellous what good order the Mounted Police keep on this side of the Rockies. Every kind of work falls to their lot. The Inspector told me that on their list of men either lost or wanted, they have three or four hundred names. Hardly a day passes without their getting some communication requesting them to trace men who have entirely disappeared.

We receive a certain number of these letters also. Only the other day, a distracted mother in California wrote to me, asking if any of us could give her information about her son, of whom she had heard nothing for nearly eighteen months. He was last seen in a construction camp somewhere in the mountains. She understood he had made some money, and feared he had been robbed or murdered. Far more likely, the police said, that he had skipped the country through money difficulties, and would eventually turn up at his home in California.

Last spring, a man called Linton set out from Edson for Grande Prairie. The day after his departure a post-card was received by his relations in Edmonton signed with his name but not written in his handwriting, saying he was starting. From that day to this he has never been heard of. Probably he was drowned in crossing one of the rivers, or else hopelessly lost, or possibly there was some foul play.

I got back home long after midnight. The shack was even colder than outside. Everything that could freeze was frozen. It was 2 A.M. before the place was really warm, and I had made myself some cocoa.

I am glad to say the police have caught the bootlegger who troubled us here last week. A large amount of whisky (or what was called whisky—in reality some poisonous concoction) was brought down from the West, and introduced here in large gasoline tins. The result was heavy drinking in the bunkhouses and a free fight. One fellow called another the " son of a Dago bastard," and then the fat was in the fire. Bootleggers should be strung up and flogged.

Yesterday I spent visiting some of the homesteaders, who, in spite of the roughness of the land, have begun to settle in the vicinity of Marlboro.

The first man I called on is an old-timer for these parts, having squatted on his place over six years ago. He has better land than anyone else—his shack showed signs of having been smothered in summer with creeping plants, and he grows beautiful vegetables. For many years he was butler to the late Lord Leconfield, and was most amusing in his comparisons between English and American manners.

I had dinner with a delightful old couple who had come out here from Lancashire late in life.

" And how was it you did not come before ? " I asked.

" 'Cos I never had the money. I was a cotton

A RAILWAY-ENGINEER'S MOVING HOME IN THE MOUNTAINS

INTERIOR OF ENGINEER'S TENT

FORDING RIVER ON THE WAY TO CHURCH
(Clothes in the Bag)

weaver at 35*s.* a week in a country place, working at a mill, but I was discharged, and when you're discharged in a country place, well, you've got to move, that's all. I sold my poultry and all my stuff, and altogether we had close on £100."

"But what made you come to Canada?" I said.

"Why, 'cos I always heard it was a fine country with lots of free land. I had had my bellyful of weaving, and I thinks to myself, 'I'll go out and try my luck, and take the Missis.' So out we came last May, and booked to Calgary. I had a brother in the East, but he didn't seem to be making any more than me in the old country, so I makes up my mind to come West. Well, when we gets to Calgary, I falls in with a young Nottingham fellow, and he says to me, 'I'm going up to Edmonton to look for land,' and I says to him, 'I'll come too.' So off we goes, and fetches up here."

"And why did you choose land here?"

"Well, we looked at a map, and sees it marked 'wooded country, good land,' and we thought it would be fairly open land, with perhaps a plantation here and there. But we begins walking north of here, and it was *all* a plantation. We *were* disgusted, and I says to Missis, 'Well, we'll go back somewhere near the cement plant, and live there. They say as how there's plenty of work to be had.' And so we settled down here, and I'm earning 2.75 dollars (11*s.*) a day at the Plant. But when I wanted to rent a shack in the camp, they wanted five dollars a month for a hencoop of a place—it was only 12 by 12 feet—and we'd get a four-roomed cottage for the same money in England. And they're right, too, who told us that the living's awful dear. Coal oil is forty cents a gallon, and in England only sevenpence; flour is dearer, but Missis says as how it's richer, and onions, best Spanish onions, five pounds for fourpence on the market at Manchester, but out here 20 cents (9½*d.*) a pound. But still, don't you make no mistake, Canada's fine. Why, the climate is that good and clear, it's like Blackpool always. If only I'd come out twenty years ago!"

"Do you ever mean to go back to England?"

"In five years we'll have saved enough to go home and show 'em how we are, but I'll never work in the old country again. Why, I think of writing to the papers, and just telling some of the fellows, *many* of 'em working at twelve cents an hour, how they can earn three times as much out here."

This man used to sing in his church choir in England, but out here, though always extremely friendly and hospitable, and willing to help on the cause indirectly in every way, he seldom comes to any service. I don't know what it is about the West. So often the men seem to drop religion. They make a new start in more senses than one. I do not think it is that the Church does not train her children on sufficiently definite lines, but rather that she does not train them not to be ashamed of what they believe.

Passing a deserted shack not far from here, I saw some letters scrawled on the door, and managed to make out the two words, "Purgatory Lodge." What volumes they spoke for the torments of isolation experienced by some wretched man who had lived there!

"Baching" drives men crazy. There was a case of it at Roydale. A young Englishman, new to the district, who was formerly a bombardier in the army, went off his head and blew out his brains with a gun. Such cases are not frequent, and with the continual influx of settlers isolation becomes less likely every year. Nevertheless one comes across breakdowns of this kind occasionally.

Some five years ago, when the G.T.P. had scarcely run a trial (survey) line through the country, three adventurous Englishmen might have been found living on the banks of the McCleod River not many miles from here. Somewhat farther west dwelt a Frenchman all alone. One of the settlers from the river, hearing he was ill, went up to see if he could be of any help. He slept the night with the Frenchman, who seemed to act in a curious way, continually gripping his rifle. Next morning he appeared better, and the Englishman left, after vainly trying to persuade the foreigner to accompany him.

A few days later the Frenchman appeared, rifle in hand, drove the three friends from their shack on the Flats at the point of his loaded weapon, and took possession of the house himself, threatening to shoot anyone who came near. He had gone stark, staring mad. The three homesteaders were forced to take refuge in the bush. It was the depth of winter, and 30 below zero. They were scantily clothed, and had no provisions, nor could any be procured at that time nearer than Edmonton, 150 miles distant. They endured this state of affairs for close on two days, till they were almost dead with fatigue and cold. Then they called the madman from the house by a subterfuge, got their guns, and shot him dead.

HEAD OF STEEL, AND BEYOND

MARLBORO, ALBERTA,
November 3rd.

I HAVE just returned from a trip into the construction camps beyond the end of steel.

About a week ago, I went down to Edson to see Provis and to get my mail, and went straight out west from there. The passenger trains run at night now, which is a fearful business, as it means we are up at all hours of the night a good many times every week. The 10 P.M. out of Edmonton arrives at Edson at 4.15 in the morning, and pulls out again at 4.35. I got up shortly after 3.30, and was down at the station in good time.

Imagine my disgust to find out from a passing switchman that the train was about three hours late, and would not be in before seven. There was no one about except twenty Galicians, who were lying or rolling about the platform, all drunk. I went back again to the shack, and lay down partly dressed. At 7 o'clock I returned to the station, and found the train was not now expected until 8.30. I again returned, and had some breakfast. Then I went back to the station, and the train finally came in at about 9.30 —over five hours late.

Of course there is nothing remarkable in trains being five hours late on a newly constructed line, but it is trying when one has to get up at unearthly hours of the night. We made a quick run to Fitzhugh, making up about one and a half hours, and arriving there about 2 P.M.

I stayed at Beecham's this time; they were most kind. I was given a little bedroom, and told I should be welcome to all meals.

To live and work on the direct line of these two great Transcontinental Railways is wonderfully interesting. It is always a matter of speculation as to whom one is going to meet next, and the feverish activity of the work, which seems to continue unabated day and night, summer and winter, is very stimulating. For instance, when one spends a few days in Fitzhugh or at some point farther west, one gets into close touch with everything that is going on. The continually changing crowds of men, here to-day and gone to-morrow, who are to be found any day round the Beechams' table, are a queer and interesting bunch.

Certainly if you asked each man who he was and what he was there for, you would have a curious list. Here, for instance, is a journalist, who has been touring the West investigating graft in over-subdivided towns, and is now having a

FITZHUGH RAILWAY STATION, NOVEMBER 1912,
WITH ONE OF THE BREWSTER BOYS IN FOREGROUND

look at the end of steel, so as to give his readers in Eastern Canada an idea as to what is going on. His neighbour at the table is Foley, Welsh & Stewart's chief paymaster at Mile 53, and he hands out thousands of dollars' worth of cheques every week.

The next man is a tie contractor,[1] who has several camps out west in the bush, busy getting out ties for the steel laying. Next to him is a young Englishman, who has been working all summer on the prairie for the C.N.R., and has now come to work in the mountains because it is warmer. He is waiting word to go right away west of Tête Jaune Cache to the Albreda Pass, which the C.N.R. crosses on its way south-west to Vancouver. Next to him is an old fellow who looks rather like a retired Colonel; he is a contractor, and has a camp of 200 men not many miles distant. Next to him sits a keen-featured Yankee; he travels up and down between Winnipeg and the end of steel in charge of the different bunches of men who are always being forwarded to the front from Winnipeg, Eastern Canada, and the States. He makes a long trip about once a week. Every big bunch of men has a "man-catcher" of this sort in charge. Next to him is a well-known prospector, bronzed and weather-beaten after a summer and autumn

[1] *i.e.* he owns one or more camps where the men are employed in felling trees and making sleepers.

in the mountains. He is now returning to civilisation to register the claims he has staked. Next to him is a member of a well-known firm of druggists, who have branches all over the West, and he is here to have a look round for further business openings. The talk, of which there is sometimes surprisingly little, is mostly railway talk, but not the less interesting for that.

I visited the hospital, where there were several typhoid cases. One of the men I saw there had been cooking in a camp out West. He had served his apprenticeship as a baker at Marlborough (England) in the College bakeries. Any man, if he can make good bread, pastry and cakes, could easily become a cook out here in the camps, and earn high wages. It would not take him long to learn to cook meat and vegetables, and it is good bread and pies that the men insist on.

Supper with Mrs. Hamilton, and then across to the round-house (*i.e.* semicircular building with stalls for the locomotives) to see the men. I found only three I knew, the others had all changed. That is one of our chief difficulties in the West. Work is plentiful, and if a man is not absolutely satisfied, off he goes. All of the men were earning good wages—far better wages than I could get. It is one of the remarkable features of this country that a skilled labourer can probably earn far more money than a man who has had an expensive education. It is very noticeable when one finds machinists earning 45 to 50 cents an hour, and putting in as many as 400 hours a month. Of course this is exceptional, and means terrifically hard work. The ambition of two of these fellows was to make enough money to bring in an income of £150 a year, and then to settle down with a little farm in England. I wonder whether they will ever do it.

The next day, being Sunday, we had a splendid service: not nearly all came who I hoped would, but the room was well filled. The following morning I went West. It was an indescribably beautiful journey. There can be no doubt at all that the glory of the West is the "fall" of the year, when the days are absolutely clear and the sun shines brilliantly in an unclouded sky. The leaves of the millions upon millions of poplar trees turn a bright gold; the wet swampy growth of the muskeg reddens. The mass of yellow foliage, the crimson tints of the undergrowth, the brilliance of the sky and the piquancy of the air, which, for all the warmth of the sun, has an unmistakable foretaste of winter in it, make the Canadian autumn, in my opinion, the pleasantest time in the whole year. It was just such a morning as this that I travelled over the Yellowhead Pass and down to Tête Jaune Cache.

When we had passed Mile 29, we came to the best piece of scenery on the whole line. From Mile 29 to Mile 45 it is exquisite. Mount Robson is the highest peak in the whole range; it is about 13,700 feet, and with its great rock walls, ribbed and scarred by ancient glacial pressure, dominates the situation. Imagine the beauty of steaming down the valley on such a morning. The grade has been literally hewn out of the rocky side of the mountains. Below are the foaming waters of the Fraser; opposite, the hills are a billowy mass of yellow interspersed with dark patches of spruce and pine; above, tower rocky peaks; and at the end of the valley rise the gigantic precipices of Mount Robson.

About 2 P.M. we reached Mile 52, *i.e.* Tête Jaune Cache. It is the present head-of-steel town, composed of people who have followed the line right along. You would have found many of them at Entwistle, Wolf Creek, Bickerdike, Hinton, and Mile 29. It is the usual medley of shacks and tents, pool rooms and stores, a barber's shop, and all the other accompaniments, good and bad, of such a community. The valley is open and well wooded.

A mile farther on are Foley, Welsh & Stewart's headquarters. They will not have the town, and all the rowdyism it brings, near their offices and stores. At Mile 53 one sees brought to perfection the art of feeding an army of men, who are living in camps situated from 20 to 90 miles down the Fraser River. Lining the south bank of the river, which is navigable for steamers up to

MILE 53, B.C.: FOLEY, WELSH, AND STEWART'S HEADQUARTERS

this point, is a long wharf, and flanking this is an enormous warehouse some two hundred or three hundred yards long. This gigantic storeroom is made of logs, but has a canvas roof—all the temporary camp buildings are put up on this system. On the other side of it are drawn up a row of box-cars, out of which are being unloaded provisions and necessaries of all kinds—sacks of flour, potatoes, vegetables, sugar, huge tins of lard, jam, rice, cases of dried fruits, kegs of nails, bales of wire, tons of material of every description, packed high to the roof on either side. Down the middle from end to end runs a narrow gangway, along which harassed clerks hurry this way and that, with bundles of paper in hand, checking the various things as they are brought in or taken out. Everything is shipped up on the train straight from Edmonton, and then either "cached" in the warehouse or loaded straight on to the scows and floated down the river to the various camps.

The scows are made out of new lumber, and in shape are not unlike barges, though they are pointed and not curved at each end. Two great oars, one at the stern and the other at the bow, are the means of steering these unwieldy-looking craft; the current, of course, carries them down. The scows never return, but are broken up for lumber when they reach their destination. From here onwards, there are camps dotted along the river bank practically the whole way to Fort George.

The whole problem of feeding the men has been immeasurably simplified by the presence of the river. Instead of spending enormous sums on paying freighters for hauling their stuff over many miles of unspeakable trail—from the head of steel up to the front—the freight is simply floated down the river. True, the Fraser is treacherous, but it is worth the risk. Of course this means of transportation is at an end now as winter is nearly here, and freighting with sleighs will soon be in progress. The ice on the Fraser, however, has the reputation of being rather "punky" (*i.e.* rotten).

Mile 53 is certainly a marvel of organisation. Besides the huge warehouses and other offices belonging to Foley, Welsh & Stewart, all the various sub-contractors have their offices there as well. The sub-contractors get their provisions from Foley, which is the only practical scheme, as each small contractor could not possibly freight in just his own stuff. Transportation of this kind has to be done on a large scale, if it is to be done at all.

My first duty on arriving at Tête Jaune was to visit Charlie Baker, a coloured man, who had been working at Fitzhugh in the station restaurant. He and his wife had been to several of our services, and, like so many coloured people, they possess a highly developed religious vein. Charlie has made a success of life. He used to be in the theatrical line, and made big money at it, but, tired of the life, he took up his former trade of barber, and he and his wife moved out West. They have two tents at Tête Jaune, one to live in, and one fitted up as a bath-house and barber's shop. Charlie was anxious "to start a little Bible Class, and to sing a few sacred songs." For this reason I had brought him up one or two Bible-study papers, some Bibles, and also a little book on the study of the New Testament.

I found him putting the finishing touches to his brown canvas tents.

"Hullo, Charlie, how are you?"

"Fine and dandy, Reverend, and how's yourself?"

"Fine, thanks. I've just come in on the train, and I've brought along some Bibles and study papers for you."

"Say now, ain't that dandy? I'm awful obliged to you."

I produced the books and papers.

"Say now, I'm just tickled to death over them books. Shan't we have some times readin'? I'm figuring on startin' right in on Sunday. You'll be here, Reverend, eh?"

"I'm afraid not, Charlie. I'm going west now, and when I'm through I'll have to get right back east to Marlboro."

"You're going to hit the trail right now? Why! The mud's a fright, and you'll have an awful hike."[1]

"I'm going to make ten miles at any rate to-night, so I guess I'd better hustle."

"Now, wait a minute! Will you let me do you a favour, Reverend?"

"What do you mean, Charlie?"

"Well, will you let me?" he persisted.

"What is it?"

"Say now, Reverend, have you got any gloves?"

"Yes," I said, and pulled them out.

"Nay, nay, them are no good," he said; and, before I knew where I was, he had me by the arm, and we were walking down the street (if it can be dignified with such a title) of Tête Jaune Cache.

I was ushered into a wonderful log shanty, bearing a placard outside with "General Store" roughly scrawled on it. Inside, piled high on the rough plank counter, lining the walls up to the roof, hanging from the logs, and taking up a good deal of the floor space, were goods of every description. Behind the counter sat a particularly big man chewing tobacco and spitting. He was dressed in a red shirt and kerchief and dark breeches.

"Say, Mick, this is the Reverend. Now he's

[1] "Hike," western slang for a long tramp on foot.

going west o' here to-night, and he ain't got any gloves—at least none as are any good, so I'm going to buy him a pair. Just let's have a look at your best."

Mick got up slowly, as if it was great condescension to serve us at all, and shoved a heap of gloves and mits in front of us.

"I guess these are good," he said, and held up a splendid sheepskin-lined pair.

I remonstrated, knowing they were expensive, but Charlie grinned all over his face, and decided that I should have them at once.

"What's the best camp to make to-night?" I said to Mick.

"Why, 62 or 66 I would think. Just come in?"

"Yes, just got off the train."

"Well, you'll have to get a move on," he said, "if you're going to make that far to-night. The grade's pretty mushy for walking, and it gets dark soon. A preacher came to one of the camps I was in once," he added, and then, with extreme sarcasm, "a darned fine preacher he was! Got lousy I guess—never came back anyway!" and Mick paid no more attention to us.

I then started off west without further delay, passing two men struggling under several heavily laden grips (suit-cases) which obviously contained drink. They had been brought up on the train. You might as well try to stop the wind from blowing as prevent bootlegging. While there's money in bringing it in, and while the men want it, the thing will be done.

Half a mile or so beyond Foley's headquarters, I passed the actual head of steel. The two rails simply came to an end, and a couple of ties were thrown loosely across. The grade continued right along by the Fraser. About dusk I hit a good-sized camp, situated right on the banks of the Fraser. On the dump were toiling and sweating some eighty or ninety men. A steam shovel was ladling out huge chunks of clay, and depositing them in the little trucks drawn by a noisy "dinky-engine." Some of the men were engaged in looking after this work, others were working with pick and shovel up to their knees in mud. Mud! well I never have seen such stuff. In a second it was over into my boots; and my overalls up to the knees were absolutely yellow and reeking wet with it. I sloshed through it all, and made for the log shanty which was evidently the office. A tall cadaverous-looking clerk was engaged in signing papers and cheques. I waited till he looked up, and then asked if I could stay the night, telling him who I was.

"Sure you can," he said, "if you can find a bunk. We have 120 men working here, and there's always a big bunch over-night going east or west. You'd better get a bunk at once."

"Could you fix me up with a blanket?"

GROUP OF RAILWAY "BOSSES" AT FITZHUGH

THE "DUMP"
(Constructing a high embankment)

INTERIOR OF TYPICAL BUNK-HOUSE
(Notice spruce pole bunks)

"I guess so. Wait a minute." And he kindly fished me one out from somewhere.

Owing to slides from the grade, the bunkhouses, which consisted of three tents, had been placed on some rising ground above. I went into one tent. The bunks, built of spruce poles, lined the two long sides, and were indescribably dirty. They all seemed to be occupied, and I was glad, because the place had an extremely evil smell. I gave up the quest till after supper, of which I felt in need, having had nothing since breakfast at Fitzhugh.

We had supper in an immense log cook-shack. There must have been 200 of us and more. There was plenty of food on the table, but unless one was very hungry it would be difficult to eat a good meal, because the conditions under which it is served are distinctly unattractive. One man sticks his fork into the potatoes, another puts the spoon he has just had in his mouth into the sugar, or dumps a dirty plate right down on to the cake. Everyone eats as if his life depended on it, only raising his head to ask his neighbour to pass something else.

Supper over, we trooped out into the mud and slush. The ascent to the bunkhouses, which the slippery clay and fearful mud made a matter of real difficulty, was attended with some of the worst blasphemy I have ever heard. I went into one bunkhouse, which I had been told by a friendly teamster was mostly occupied by English-speaking fellows.

" How's chance for a bunk, boys ? "

" Mighty poor. I guess we're full up."

I said nothing, but began distributing magazines and illustrated papers.

" Say, I guess I haven't got the price for these papers," said one ; " how much ? "

" They're free."

" Well, what do you know about that ? Say, you're not such a bad guy either."

I told them what my work was.

" Now, why didn't you say that before, Parson ? Why, sure there's room. I guess you can double up with Harry. He looks after the lamps, and he'll be in presently."

I felt grateful, though if it had not been cold and wet, how much I should have preferred to sleep outside ! The bunkhouse was long, but narrow. The bunks, of which there were two tiers, ran down both sides, and only left a very narrow aisle in the middle. At the far end was a heater, and we all sat at that end facing each other on two benches, while quite a few preferred to lie in their bunks.

I wish you could have seen those men. They came in covered with mud from head to foot, and proceeded to divest themselves of their wet boots and socks and overalls, which they hung up from every conceivable corner. Some put on dry socks, but most stayed with bare feet. The floor was soon as muddy as it was outside, with men coming in and out, and, of course, everyone spat where they wished. When you see the conditions under which these men live, you could hardly be surprised if the outlook which many of them have on life is little better than a beast's. They work like horses, eat like pigs, and sleep like logs. Is it to be wondered at that after months of this they go wild when they reach the lights and glare of a city, and that the height of enjoyment is to be found in the whisky bottle?

The foreigners stay longest with this kind of work. The English-speaking men go from one job to another, and seldom seem to stay any length of time in any one camp. The pay is not bad; in the fall, when there are other attractions such as harvesting, they can get three dollars (12*s.*) a day, out of which they pay one dollar (4*s.*) a day for board. There are a few other charges, such, for instance, as the three-dollar poll tax, which each man, if he works only for twenty-four hours in British Columbia, has to pay to the Government of that province. There is also a charge of one dollar a month for doctor and twenty-five cents a month for mail.

A good part of the evening we talked and smoked. There were men of all sorts in that bunkhouse. To start with, I found myself sitting next to an old Scotchman who had come from near Aberfoyle. Having motored through that country on the way to Loch Awe, I knew the place. Behind me, lying in a bunk, was a young fellow who had been studying medicine at Edinburgh, but had come to grief in some way or other. He wanted to know, in a perfectly refined voice, if I did not find it a bit rough travelling through the camps. He was a man whom in the old country we should call a gentleman. Above him was another fellow who was running one of Foley, Welsh & Stewart's scows on the Fraser. He was well educated, knew Latin, and had been through a High School; his ambition was to get to the University one day.

To call these men "navvies," in the English sense of the word, is quite a mistake. They are nothing of the kind. Of course some are merely rough labourers; the foreigners, for instance, are often a somewhat degraded lot; but the majority are men who are making a grubstake, or who have come down in the world. Regular "hoboes" they look. But had you seen me, I doubt whether you would have thought me much better—covered with mud as I was from head to foot, with some old overalls, a very ancient jacket, and a battered old hat.

Before turning in we had a service, in the course of which I read to them from the New Testament. Before I had finished, one old fellow whom I had noticed fumbling in a box at the end of his bunk, produced a very aged Bible. He found the place, and pushed it towards me saying, "Here, Parson, read that; it'll do the boys good to hear it."

He had chosen the story of Susannah from the Apocrypha. I looked at him sharply, but saw he was serious. I therefore read it, and the men all listened intently. At the end I pointed a moral, and I hope the old fellow was right—that it *did* do some good.

At last it was time to go to "bed"! Harry had turned up, and proved to be an Englishman from Putney. His father drives a Vanguard 'bus from Putney to the Bank. All the bunks were double, and he said I could certainly sleep with him. He had a blanket, and so had I, so we shared the two. I took off coat and overalls, and slept in my underclothing, making a pillow of my muddy clothes; it was all I had. The bunk had a little straw in it.

Directly above us, with the straw of their bed sticking through the spruce poles, slept two Galicians, who, I must say, appeared to be perfectly filthy.

"Say, Parson, I'm not lousy," said Harry, "but I can't answer for them darned Galicians above."

The men generally sleep in the shirts and underpants they have been wearing all day, and I don't think they wash them very often. Harry and I talked quite a bit before going to sleep; and then he snored, and I had a wretched night —it sleeted and blew outside, and the pines sounded very dreary. I was glad when it was time to get up at 6.30. Hurriedly putting on our muddy things of the night before (no one showed any signs of washing), we stumbled down through the slippery darkness to breakfast.

Next morning I went on down the valley to several other camps. But I must not weary you with the tale. Everywhere there were signs of the greatest activity. The grade is a regular highway—continual coming and going. At one place I must have passed fifty or sixty men of all nationalities, each with his pack or grip on his shoulders, marching two by two, looking for a job. The foreigners are ignorant and often deceived. I met one man who was French and had lost his friend. I asked him where he was going.

"To Vancouver," he replied.

"And how far do you think that is?" I asked.

"Why, they tell me it is only seventy miles west of here," said the poor fellow, and was much bewildered when I told him the truth.

On the grade they work Sundays, week-days, summer and winter, wet or fine, unless the weather is absolutely prohibitive, which in British Columbia does not seem often to be the case. If pressed, they work at night by the light of powerful

RAFT ON THE FRASER PASSING TÊTE JAUNE CACHE

LOADING A SCOW AT TÊTE JAUNE CACHE

A TRESTLE BRIDGE ON THE C.N.R. JUST FINISHED

acetylene lamps. Railroad construction, through a vast untrodden country like this, is a gigantic undertaking—"kinks of nature made straight while you wait," as an engineer once said to me. Think of the army of men engaged on the work —thousands of labourers grading, tunnelling, and blasting; large gangs of skilled workmen trestling and bridge-building; hundreds of freighters engaged in carrying provisions and other necessaries from the head of steel into the camps; and as for the horses, I don't know how many are used for this work and on the grade itself.

It is amazing to think of the capital sunk in the necessary plant, such as steam shovels, graders, dumpcarts, scrapers, pile-drivers, track-laying machines. The initial expense of sending survey parties through miles of uninhabited country must be immense. And even when the steel has been laid there are hosts of men engaged in ballasting the track, building stations, sidings, yards, and so forth.

I got back to Mile 53 the following day at about 1.30, and walked on to Tête Jaune Cache to get some dinner. An end-of-steel town is a wicked place. Every other log shanty or tent that you see is either a gambling joint, drinking saloon, brothel, or pool room. The women make large sums of money, and are constantly going down to Edmonton to cash regular stacks of cheques. Some make 200 or 300 dollars a week.

Men come in, and give a girl a 15, 25, 30 dollar cheque for an evening, or perhaps even for a few minutes, and then go off back to the grade determined to make another stake and "blow it in" in the same way.

There were numbers of restaurants—sordid looking places most of them. I walked into one, and sat down at the lunch counter. It seemed to be frequented by women of bad character, but was clean, and the food was decently cooked and served. I got talking to the girl who served me. I looked a regular hoboe as regards my clothes, but she appeared interested in me. I asked her about herself. She also was a girl of no character, and told me that she had seen much better days, had lived in Piccadilly, and also in Paris, but her home was in Liverpool. I asked her if she knew some of our name—doctors in Rodney Street. Yes, she knew the name well, and then of course she was all agog to know what I was doing out there "in such a God-forsaken place" as Tête Jaune Cache. I asked her what she thought I was doing.

"I don't know," she said, "unless you have been a bad boy, and they've sent you out to get rid of you."

I couldn't help laughing, and for answer showed her my railroad pass, which has Mission House, Edmonton, on it. You should have seen her face. It was a picture. How so much wickedness can exist in the presence of such perfect beauty as at Tête Jaune Cache is a wonder.

Well, I must close. I got back here the following evening. The train dropped me at Dandurand at 12.30, and I got up to the shack about 1 A.M.

RAILWAY CONSTRUCTION CAMPS

MARLBORO, ALBERTA,
Jan. 15th.

I MUST try and write you some account of rather an interesting trip from which I have just returned.

I left here a week ago for Edson, travelling that far with the station agent on his speeder—an excellent machine with four small wheels, which run on the rails; it is driven by a gasoline engine. It is an extremely exhilarating way of travelling, though somewhat cold, when the temperature is below zero and the speed reaches over thirty miles an hour.

Edson seemed pretty busy. When the snow comes, the town prepares for an influx of Grande Prairie and Peace River settlers. The rivers are frozen and the trails good for sleighing, so the homesteaders from those distant parts are forced to take advantage of the few months when freighting is possible to lay in a substantial stock of provisions, and bring in farming implements or other necessaries. As soon as the "break up" comes, and rivers and muskegs thaw out, it is almost impossible for horses or oxen to pull heavy loads over the roads.

GRANDE PRAIRIE SETTLERS LEAVING EDSON

HOMESTEADERS STARTING FROM EDSON FOR THE PEACE RIVER
(Three hundred mile trip)

DOG TRAIN COMING INTO TOWN

There is something rather romantic in watching a Peace River outfit pull out from Edson on its long fifteen or sixteen days' journey. The homesteader has three to four hundred miles in front of him, and there are few stopping-places. Indeed, were there such places of shelter all along the trail, it is doubtful whether the homesteader's purse would allow him to make use of them. He has probably been into Edmonton by train, and a few days "in town," with all the delights of civilisation in the shape of theatres, picture shows, and hotel bars, have not left many spare dollars. The load too, piled high on his sleighs, represents a considerable outlay of money. No! When night overtakes the traveller, he will choose some sheltered spot for his camp, close to a creek which has not quite frozen to the bottom, build his fire at the mouth of his tent, see to his team, cook his pork and flapjacks, and roll up in his blankets till the morning.

The following day I left Edson for the West. It was snowing hard as I tramped down to the station soon after four o'clock in the morning. The train was late. The waiting-room was full of men, many of whom had slept there, and as others came in covered with snow, the atmosphere became wet and smelly. We got off about 5.30, and as we went farther west the dark snow clouds rolled away to the east and we ran into a perfect fairyland.

Everything was covered with the fresh fall of snow, the spruce trees bending under the heavy load. The Athabasca was almost frozen, just a narrow stream of black water flowing swiftly between ice banks. Then up over the heavy bank of clouds came the sun, flooding the gigantic peaks with light, till the whole range shone and glittered like a dazzling chain of jewels. The mountains have many moods, but never have I seen them more beautiful than on that morning.

At Fitzhugh we picked up more passengers for Tête Jaune. The train was well filled as usual with labouring men, of all nationalities, going to the front, as well as contractors, engineers, surveyors, drummers, and (no doubt) bootleggers. There is always a sort of buoyancy about everybody when their faces are turned towards the West. Somebody comes up and slaps you on the back with a cheery "Well, where are you hittin' for now, Parson?" or "Beating it for the West again?" Then the train agent comes along just after we have started, and shouts, "All going through to 53, boys?" and the newsagent follows with a basket of fizzy drinks, shouting "B.C. whisky, boys, B.C. whisky," or "ice-cold drinks," and somebody facetiously remarks it looks mighty like snow to him outside and we haven't reached the banana belt yet.

At the summit of the pass there was plenty of snow, and as we ran down farther into British

Columbia it became evident that there was a much heavier fall on the western slope of the mountains than on the Alberta side. On the way I ate my lunch which the restaurant people at Fitzhugh had slipped into my pack before starting—bread, meat and pie, and (kind thought) a small box of cigarettes.

At Mile 49, B.C., there had sprung up a row of rooming houses, restaurants, pool rooms, shooting galleries, and general stores—all due to the fact that here the C.N.R. main line branches off from the G.T.P. and goes south-westerly over the Albreda Pass to Vancouver; it is the headquarters for the time being of some of the bigger contractors like Phelan and Shirley.

We arrived at Mile 53 at about two o'clock, and I tried to find out if a work train was likely to be leaving for the West that night. The work train comes up most nights to get ties, rails, and other materials for the steel-laying gang. There was also a freight running as far as 71. But no one seemed to know, and I decided to hike, though it was now nearly three o'clock and I knew it must be a matter of twenty miles before I could hope to reach the steel-laying gang, which might be anywhere between Mile 69 and 79.

I had gone about four miles when a fellow on a gasoline speeder overtook me. I stopped him in the most barefaced way and asked for a lift.

"Sure, if you take chances of being thrown

off," he said; "the track hasn't been laid many days."

And certainly it was rough going. The steel rails rose and fell in proper switchback fashion, and time and again we had to slacken the engine to allow us to go over a particularly bad spot. But the engine evidently disliked this treatment, and began to show signs of giving out. I therefore insisted on walking again, as I knew he would probably make it with just his own weight. However, the lift of three or four miles had helped me a great deal.

I was now tramping along by the side of the newly-laid steel, through big timber, the frozen river below me on the right, and the high wooded hills of the Fraser Valley rising on both sides.

About 5.30 I struck a stopping-place—at 64, I think—and was joined by another hiker also making for 71. It was seven o'clock and quite dark before we came round a corner through a cut, and almost walked into the rear car of a train. The train consisted of a huge string of box-cars (like the heavy English goods wagons, but much larger), each of them converted by the insertion of a door and a couple of small square windows into a bunkhouse on wheels. It seemed of interminable length. A group of men with lanterns informed us that this was the steel-laying gang. Near the middle of it were two large dining-cars, neither of which had seen a coat of paint for many a long year. To clamber up by a little wooden ladder was a difficult matter in the dark; but, though supper was long over, I decided I must brave the cook's wrath, and get something to eat and drink.

I walked through the first dining-car into the kitchen, and found a big brawny-armed cook just surveying his completed labours with satisfaction.

"Cook, how's the chance for a cup of tea?"

"Damn you! Do you think a cook's never through?" he said, and went off into an unusually long flow of oaths.

"Look here," I replied at last, "I've just had a hike of twenty miles carrying a pack of magazines and papers for you and the men, and I tell you straight if I could get a little supper I'd be real glad."

He didn't budge an inch.

"I guess you're a preacher, then, ain't you? Yes, I thought so. Well, just listen, young man. I work—I don't preach."

"Is that so? I do both."

Silence for a few moments. "Well, I guess you'll find some tea on the stove," he drawled out at last, "and I'll get you something to eat if you wait."

Not long afterwards he fetched out a pair of spectacles which made him look quite benign, and, turning over the pages of *Pearson's Magazine*, wanted to know all about our work. He told me he had a gang of 200 men to feed, and had an assistant cook and six cookees. He had followed rail-roading a good part of his life, and was amusing about the various Englishmen he had seen working on the grade. At one camp where he was cooking last summer some Englishmen dressed in comparatively good clothes had turned up to work on the grade.

"I tell you it was great," he chuckled, "to see them dudes[1] with their swell suits and patent leather boots ridin' on the dump wagons."

Having found out from the cook the name of the boss, and in which car he was, I went off to find him. After several bad shots, I clambered into one car, and found a number of men smoking and writing. The place was fitted up partly as bunkhouse and partly as office.

"Mr. Lowe?"

"Sure, that's me."

I told him who I was, and asked him if I could stay the night and see the men.

"Why, sure," he said, "stay as long as you like, and you can have a bunk in the Commissary's car. That'll be cleaner than among the men. You'll find them a tough bunch to convert, though!"

The timekeeper, I found, was an old friend of mine, and he volunteered to walk down to the other end of the train with me and fix up matters

[1] Western slang for a dandy.

"GRADING" NEAR MARLBORO

The grader drawn by eight horses ploughs up the soil, which is forced up the shoot into the dump wagons

(See the photograph opposite p. 224)

with the Commissary. We found the Commissary playing poker with a number of other men, and he readily consented to put me up. I then felt free to go round and visit the men. Nearly half the gang were foreign-speaking. As I went down the train, I listened carefully to the various sounds coming from each box-car. Foreigners always herd together if possible, and the English-speaking fellows do not care to have much to do with them.

The first car I climbed into was fixed up as a blacksmith's shop, and the smith was blowing his fire in one corner. Both he and his assistant proved to be English. The smith came from Exeter. They were highly delighted with the magazines, and we had a chat about Devonshire, which led on to deeper subjects. The next car was very filthy in appearance. Four men were playing poker, and a good many more lying about, some in their bunks, others on the floor smoking and spitting. I had not been in there long before one fellow, who was French, began singing one of the filthiest songs I have ever heard. The others nudged him, but he professed not to understand—at any rate he took no notice—neither did I. It is quite useless to ask them to stop. A great deal of it is done just to see what one will say, and if one says nothing the joke is a failure, and the fellow, who is quite likely a decent kind of chap at heart, stops of his own accord, and takes care not to repeat it when you are there again.

The language in the camps is the foulest that I have ever heard (even beating that of the Inns of Court squadron when we had to "stand to horses" at 1.0 A.M. on a pouring wet night on Salisbury Plain!). Another car I entered was occupied almost entirely by English fellows, several of them old navy men. You should have seen how they rushed at me when I announced I had stuff to read. One fellow thought they were tracts, and said he didn't want any. I laughed, and said nothing. But when he saw a bundle of the latest American and English illustrated magazines he altered his cry, and elbowed his way through the crowd to get some.

"Say, are you going to stay here to-night?" said one of the men.

"Sure."

"Well, I guess you'll go away a bit heavier than you came. This place is just crawling."

"It's waste of energy and time to keep clean," added another as he viciously scratched himself.

"Well, it wouldn't be the first time I've had company," I said; "but as a matter of fact I've got a bunk with the Commissary."

We chatted and talked mostly about railroading, and the kind of life they and I were leading, and then before saying good-night I suggested reading the Bible and having a few prayers. Of

GRAND TRUNK PACIFIC LOCOMOTIVE, WITH TONY OKE, CONDUCTOR, AND CREW, TÊTE JAUNE CACHE, NOVEMBER 1912

course one never quite knows how this will be taken. There are generally one or two of the men who have the courage to say "Sure, do!" There are always a number who secretly acquiesce and are even pleased, though they are shy and remain silent; and there are generally a few who profess to take no interest whatever, and blatantly continue their former occupation. However, this time there were none of the latter class, and quite a number openly said they would like it. One particularly nice-looking fellow spoke up. "Sure," he said, "you read it! We don't often hear the Bible nowadays. Jim, up there"—and he pointed to a fellow sprawling on one of the upper bunks—"has got one somewhere stowed away in his pack. I guess it don't often see the light, though."

And so I read to them from St. Matthew, and though I didn't attempt to preach we had some good talk on the passage, after which I said the General Confession, and we had some other prayers. I do not for one moment imagine that they will not probably tell obscene stories, and use just the same vile oaths as soon as I have clambered down out of the car; but at any rate I for one shall treasure the memory of that service in the box-car down the Fraser Valley among the happiest and certainly the most interesting of my associations with the West.

There were several bunks in the Commissary's

car. Besides himself and his clerk, about four of the cookees appeared to sleep there. I half undressed, and slipped into the blankets, but slept badly, owing to the fearful heat of the car. There was a coal-heater, and it was burning furiously all night. Unfortunately, I had a bunk very near it.

Next morning at five o'clock, an engine, which had been shunting up and down for several hours, gave a long hoot, and we all hastily donned our overalls and tumbled down on to the track, and found our way along the train and up into the dining-car. No one washes except possibly on Sundays; there are no facilities for it, and, with the train constantly moving a few miles every other day or two, it is often a difficult matter in winter to get even sufficient drinking-water.

The night before, numbers of camp-fires on the wooded slopes above and below had made a most picturesque effect. They belonged to freighters, who were freighting stuff from there right down to the Canyon, and these were now just beginning to get under way. There are thousands of teams on the trail just now between Tête Jaune Cache and Fort George.

Shortly after breakfast, the huge locomotive pulled up alongside our train, pushing in front of it several flat cars piled high with ties and rails, immediately behind it being an old coach which would long ago have been on the scrap heap had not this further use been found for it. I scrambled up into the coach with the men, and quickly secured an old barrel to sit on; there were no seats and late comers had to stand. There we were packed pretty tight—all smoking, most of us spitting; outside pitch dark; inside, the only light a flickering lantern at the far end; men of every age, nationality and class, unshaven, dirty, and, at this time of the morning, fairly silent.

Suddenly the train gave a great jerk, and, with much cursing and swearing, everybody was thrown against everybody else. Then we started lurching along the mile and a half of track they had laid the day before. I found myself among several of my friends of the previous night, and we chatted away. Of course a newly laid track is bad—it couldn't be anything else, when the ties (sleepers) are laid straight down on the grade, with no levelling or ballasting, and the steel rails merely fastened to them by a few spikes, but on the whole the G.T.P. is a wonderfully laid line. An enormous amount of money and time has been spent in securing a really good grade. The cuts and fills are all brought up to the required standard, and this must pay in the end, though the initial outlay is very great.

On arriving at the end we all tumbled out into the snow, of which there must have been about three feet, and walked along the flat cars. These were now coupled to the "pioneer," which was standing at the head of the long train of material on the very last piece of steel, laid the night before. It was of course quite dark, and we only had the light of the lanterns which the foremen carried.

The first thing was to erect the two trams, one on either side of the train. Each tram consists of two parallel steel beams joined together by rollers about every eight feet. These steel beams are fixed to the train by brackets; the rollers which they support revolve at a great pace, and automatically carry forward on one side of the train the ties, and on the other side the rails. Both of these are thus rapidly propelled from the back of the train to the very front of the pioneer. The height of each tram from the ground is about the same as that of the flat cars to which it is attached. Men stand on the flat cars, and feed the trams with ties and rails. But as the train goes up to Tête Jaune Cache every night for fresh material, the trams have to be detached and laid on the ground at the end of each day's work. The first duty was therefore to get them into place. I had, as a matter of fact, intended going on at once farther west, but, just as I was starting off, one of the foremen shouted out, "Here, you fellow, come and give us a hand with the trams," which I was only too glad to do. So had you been there, you might have seen me sweating away with one of the roughest bunches of men at that time in the West—a steel-laying gang being by reputation as tough a bunch as you would find anywhere. We all lined up facing the cars—at least our party did, there were two parties, one working on each side of the train—then, when the brackets were properly fixed, the foreman gave the word, and with one big heave we had raised the first section of the tram into place; and so we went on down to the end of the train, fitting each section into the last, till the whole was completed. I was covered with oil and dirt by the time we had finished, but it was certainly an amusing and quite a unique experience! By this time it was getting light, and it was highly interesting to gain a practical knowledge of the whole process of laying steel.

First there is the grade, which is left ready and comparatively level by the contractors, although a great deal of ballasting and levelling up is necessary after the steel is laid. The important thing is to get the rails down, no matter how, so that the supplies can be forwarded by train to the nearest point to the camps. About half a mile ahead of the pioneer come the surveyors, who stake out the line, putting in centre stakes, which are the only guide the steel-layers have to go by. Then in this case, it being winter, came twenty or thirty men shovelling away the heavy snow. Then the pioneer itself, which looks more like a large crane placed on a truck than anything else. From two long steel arms, placed at an angle of about 45 degrees, hang steel ropes which catch the rails as they come off the tram. Men rush forward, bear them down into place, and join them up to the last two already laid—the exact breadth of the gauge is given by a man with a properly measured rod. No spikes are driven until later. Before this stage, the ties, which fairly hurtle off the tram on the other side of the train, have been caught, each one by two men, and placed in position far enough for one or two lengths of rail—then the tiemen stand aside, and, as I have described, the railmen place the rails in position. After two or three lengths of rail have been laid in this way, the pioneer gives two short hoots, the two locomotives behind give a few puffs, and the pioneer and the whole train advance some twenty or thirty feet; the pioneer then gives one hoot as a signal for the train to stop. The trams are again put into motion, the ties and rails again begin flying to the front, and are caught, each in turn, by the waiting men, and the whole process is put through once more.

Some fifty yards behind the train comes the gang of spikers, who drive the spikes into the ties. The protruding head of the spike, as it is driven in, catches the edge of the rail and clamps the whole thing down fast to the tie. The first gang drive in spikes at various specified intervals, and then there come along a final gang who drive in all that are left.

That night I reached another camp about 5 P.M., and went straight to the boss's tent—the "office" as it is called in these construction camps, where the timekeeper and commissary clerk have their headquarters and keep the books.

The timekeeper is not employed until after very careful inquiry into his past history. He is generally bonded by his employers with a Guarantee Company for a considerable sum, or, in other words, his honesty is insured. This is made necessary because he has a number of blank cheques handed over to him with which to pay the men. If he was dishonest, he could easily decamp with money, or through carelessness on his part a cheque could be stolen from him and his name forged. Such cheques could easily be cashed in Edmonton, as no one could be familiar with the signature of all the timekeepers.

The boss's name was Ditton, and I walked straight in and asked him if I could take some magazines round and have a "meeting" that night in the cookhouse, provided that I could persuade the cook. He gave me permission pleasantly enough, and so off I went. The cookhouse was a lumber building, and round it were congregated the tents; one was the office, the next the foreman's, then a fair-sized marquee where the teamsters lived. Beyond that, the blacksmith's shop, and still farther, a great square marquee which was the barn, the horses standing in two rows in the middle facing each other. Another tent near by was used for several mule teams, and then two or three hundred yards away was a large log bunkhouse. This was largely occupied by foreign-speaking men—Galicians, Poles, and Russians—and a few English and Americans. All these men were labourers, pick and shovel men, and were earning three dollars a day. Their board comes to about a dollar a day, but even so, with extra time, they can clear about 2.50 dollars a day, that is £3 a week—not bad for absolutely unskilled labour.

I went round, and saw everybody. It being Sunday, some had gone out "hunting," *i.e.* shooting; others were lying on their bunks smoking and talking; others, again, either washing or mending their clothes. I did my best to talk to most of them. Some appeared really pleased to see one; others quite indifferent. They were certainly a tough lot—mostly men who had been with this kind of work for a number of years. They bore the marks of their hard life in their features, and showed the lack of all civilising influences by their manners and talk.

In the large bunkhouse a furious game of poker was going on. One man I noticed in particular—a great big fellow, a Yankee I think—they called him Pat. I am afraid Pat was an inveterate gambler. The room was fair-sized, but the

RAFTING DOWN THE FRASER ON THE WAY TO FORT GEORGE

"BOOTLEGGING" UP TO DATE
(After discovery by the police)

bunks which lined it on all four sides only left a comparatively small space in the middle. Here round a rough table, were gathered a motley crew of Galicians, Russians, and English-speaking "bohuncs"[1] of every description. Some were playing, others were standing behind looking on. Pat was sitting on the farther side, and seemed in his element—his "Stettson" hat pushed to the back of his head; his face, on which grew a short stubbly beard, flushed with excitement, and a substantial heap of dollar bills in front of him.

I walked right in with the object of giving away some magazines and papers.

"Holy Jesus, what the hell do *you* want?" came from Pat in a loud voice, at which everyone looked round.

"Want? Why, I want you to stop gambling with your wages. Here's something to occupy your time a bit better."

Pat didn't quite know how to take this, but he accepted one of the magazines I held out to him.

"And who are you, anyway?" he asked.

I explained my work.

"Oh, one of these blooming sky pilots, eh?" and then, without apparently giving the matter further thought, he turned back to his cards.

"I'll go two dollars," he said, and pushed a greasy bill into the middle of the table.

[1] A rough-looking character.

I saw it was no good remonstrating at that moment, and so distributed the papers to the other men, and told them of the service that evening in the cookhouse.

Pat looked up, gave me a distinct wink, and said, "I'll be there, pilot, I'll be there!"

An hour or two later, I was going round the camp to beat up the boys, and found Pat in the "barn." It was a great square tent, with the horses standing face to face in roughly made stalls in the centre. Pat was trying to patch up some harness by the light of a lantern, and apparently found it "a mean job." He looked up as I entered.

"Say, Reverend—just get out of this tent for two minutes and let me *cuss!*"

"No, I won't, and you needn't swear this time either."

"All right," said Pat resignedly—"I guess with the 'cloth' in the barn I just can't."[1]

"Say, Pat, you promised to come to the service to-night, and we're going to start in a few minutes."

"A service? Why, God damn it! I guess I ain't been to a service for close on fifteen years."

"All the more reason for coming to-night. I guess you can make a good noise, so you'd better come and sing."

[1] Pronounced "cannt."

Pat looked puzzled. He looked at his overalls, and then at his buff-coloured shirt.

"I guess I'm none too clean," he said, and then, as if a still better excuse had come into his head:

"And I guess God Almighty don't care about a bunch of hoboes like us—anyway, what do you think, boys?" And he turned to several other teamsters who were lolling about on the bales of hay rather enjoying this dialogue.

"Gee whiz!" said one lanky fellow with a strong American drawl, "if you was to go into that meeting, I'd just think you'd gorn crazy, and that's a cinch."

We had a good service that evening. The men sang well, and listened well. At the far end of the cookhouse I saw Pat. He came in while we were singing the first hymn, and he didn't in the least look as if he'd "gorn crazy." He had contrived to tidy himself up a bit, and his features wore a very different expression to that of the poker fiend. After the service he was waiting outside.

"Well," he said, "that was just fine to hear a few hymns and a bit of the Bible again. Quite a time since I've been to church! I put a dollar into the hat anyway!" he added in a triumphant voice.

"I'm glad you enjoyed the service. The money will be used for helping on our work."

"Is that so?" said Pat, with a sly look; "well, it's better like that, I guess, than in a Galeeshan's pocket, where, I guess, it would have been right now, if I hadn't won it from him."

So much for his contribution to the collection. Poor Pat! I fear he will always gamble with every cent that comes into his possession, unless a miracle happens. But who knows? Perhaps it may.

When I got back to Mile 71, a day or two later, I found that a freight had just come in from Tête Jaune Cache, and the freighters, who had been waiting for the train, were busy loading up their wagons with bales of hay, sacks of oats and flour, cases of provisions, light steel rails, bridge timber, and every kind of stuff. Some of the teams were already pulling out, others were just arriving in.

Freighting is a fairly lucrative business, but it is a hard life. The rates paid vary a great deal. In this case each freighter was getting 3 cents for 100 lbs. per mile. Say he carries 4500 lbs., which is a good load, he therefore gets 13.50 dollars a mile, and the journey is perhaps about a hundred miles, though often less. But then, you must remember, it will take him a good many days to make the trip even without mishaps; the team must have three meals a day, and he also the same number, each of which costs him 50 cents. Even to stand the horses in a barn (without hay or oats) costs 50 cents, and the freighter has to carry his own hay and oats, which increases his load. The stopping-places are poor, the meals are often not good, and he stands to have things stolen. Yet there is money in it, and, still more, there is a strange kind of fascination about the life—the continuous travelling in the open air, the adventures of the trail, the rivalry between one team and another, the cameraderie at the various stopping-places or round the camp fire—in a word, the romance of the road.

I decided to get back to Tête Jaune Cache on the freight if possible, and showed my pass.

"Preacher? Good for you—come right in." And they were just about as nice a train crew as I ever struck. Most of the time we sat in the cupola of the caboose, which on the return journey was heading the train as the engine could not turn round, and, while we puffed along steadily the twenty intervening miles to the Cache the conductor told us about Father Pat, whom he had known very well in Rossland, B.C.

"That was a man!" he said. "He'd smoke and fight with you, and stand up and drink with you, and pray and preach as well."

This type of man undoubtedly appeals to the Westerner, though I am quite sure that the *Saint* does as much good. People have often said to me about men who have worked in this

Western country: "Such and such a man was a saint—too good for the West—and yet it did us all good to come in touch with such a good-living fellow." The thing that I notice is this. The unpractical man, the man who *makes* hardships, is not a hero but a fool. The Westerner is eminently practical, and any unnecessary expenditure of energy by the parson he looks upon as merely silly. It is not a passport to respect to feed on a handful of oatmeal and bread and tea, nor is it considered heroic to walk when one could save time and fatigue by riding, or to live in a tent in winter when a little pains and efficiency would erect a log shanty.

We were a little bit slow getting to the Cache, as the engine was "shy of water" (*i.e.* running a bit short), but on arriving I went to my usual restaurant, and had some dinner. Then a call on my coloured friend Charlie, who is making piles of money with his barber's shop and bath house (he gave me a first-class shave for nothing), a visit to some people who keep a rooming house, and so back to the station just in time to catch the train to Fitzhugh. The brakeman on the train didn't know who I was, and during the journey came and sat down next to me in a very neighbourly way.

"And so you're going out, old-timer, are you?—with your stake I guess? Got any cheques to be cashed?"

"GRADING"

The dump wagons keep pace with the grader, and when full of soil drive on to the end of the grade and dump it over

I am afraid he was disappointed when I told him I had never had a stake in my life. This cheque-cashing business is quite a thing with the train crews. They charge ten per cent. commission.

Our train was carrying the usual Western crew. Behind us were two strong healthy-looking fellows, who had been trapping up-country somewhere. There's plenty of good fur to be had for those who know how to catch it. Behind them was an Edmonton man, looking pretty smart in comparison to the rough clothes most of us were wearing. He was an insurance man, and had been travelling west to find new openings for business. I think he considered this country was a little too undeveloped as yet!

Opposite me was a curious foreign-looking man with a pointed beard. He was dressed in Western style, and was, as a matter of fact, English. He looked uncommonly ill, and was shivering; he told me that he was suffering from a periodical touch of fever which he had got in the East; and that led him on to talk of China and Japan, Australia and India, all of which countries he had lived in and knew, and now he was a sub-contractor, or something of that kind, in the Far West—Heaven knows how or why. He was an old Oxford man—Trinity, I think. Next to him was a young engineer, to whom I also got talking. He opened out a good deal over a pipe, and told me much about which I fear he would have been discreetly silent had he known what my work was.

Behind us were some regular hoboes, returning to civilisation after some months of the camps. They seemed to know a good many people along the line by name, and every new arrival that climbed on the train they greeted with a cheery "Hello, Bill!" or "Hello, Jack, how are you making it?" At one place where we stopped—one could not call it a station, there being no sign of house or habitation of any kind—a fellow clambered up who seemed to be a general favourite.

"Hello, Jimmy, how's yourself? Who'd have thought of seeing you here?"

"Fine and dandy."

"Well, where the hell have you been this last year or two?"

"Oh, doing a bit of trapping, I guess," says Jimmy. "Did some prospecting last summer too," he added.

"Staked any claims?" some one asked.

"You bet."

His hearers are interested, but not a word more is anyone going to get out of him about his summer's doings.

"Well, and where was Joe last time you saw him?"

"Joe, why I guess he's kicking the high spots

somewheres. He made a fine wad out West last winter, and went into town and blued it all, and when I last saw him he had all the G—d—d whisky between here and hell sticking out of his pocket."

And so the conversation runs on—everyone keen to know where old friends are.

"Oh, he's away down the Fraser, freighting," or "He's up in Dawson, mining." Another is on the coast, another has gone trapping, another is "packing" in the mountains, another has gone back East, "but you bet he'll be out West again soon," and so on.

It is curious how little one thinks of long tedious journeys out here. Take Thursday, for instance. I had left Mile 71 in the freight at 11 A.M., and was travelling practically incessantly till 1.30 A.M. the following morning—that is 13½ hours, and part of the time under pretty rough conditions. At home a comfortable journey from London to Aberdeen seems quite a big undertaking.

Later—January 20th.

This letter has been delayed a whole week, on account of a very sharp attack of tonsilitis in which I have been indulging. The morning after I returned from the West, I woke up feeling pretty bad, and after dinner went back to bed. I could get no thermometer, and unfortunately I had not my medicine chest with me, but I think I must have been about 102. Next day I felt rotten. But people were very kind. I must have had half the camp up here; one man cut wood, another fetched water; one lady brought cakes, another soup, another all kinds of medicines! One of the men brought me two or three eggs and some fresh milk, the latter a tremendous luxury, and worth its weight in gold. You can't imagine what eternal tinned milk is like if you are feeling ill.

I had to put off the services on Sunday. Far more people came to see me than would have dreamed of coming to church—they are all so good-hearted. Unfortunately, in this country, a sort of generous goodheartedness is supposed to be an excellent substitute for definite religion.

On Sunday night it turned very cold—about twenty degrees below zero—and although the men came up and did every conceivable thing to make me comfortable over night, yet it was extremely chilly in the shack before morning, and at five o'clock I got out of my bunk and lit the fire again, which had burnt right through. The head cook brought me up all kinds of food for dinner, which was very good of him considering he is about the busiest man in the camp. Of course there are absolutely no facilities in a shack like this for being ill, especially if it is in the winter.

MAIN STREET, TÊTE JAUNE CACHE, JANUARY 1913

There is a good deal of interest over provincial politics at the present time. There will be an election very shortly. The other day, one of the leading Liberal papers had a most caustic article on the giving of titles to Canadians, which it said must be tolerated, owing to human weakness, although it was altogether against the best interests of the country. There are many out here who are against it, as setting up the beginnings of an aristocracy. There is an old Yankee in this camp who insists on calling the Duchess of Connaught, "Mrs. Connaught"!

Provis came up here this morning. He tells me he took such a curious wedding some days ago. It was near the end of steel on the G.T.P. Alberta coal branch, and of course many miles from any church. The marriage, which took place in a shack, was between a Finn and a Swede, and was conducted by means of an interpreter. Under such circumstances any hymns were of course an impossibility. But it was evidently felt that some attempt at music ought to be made, for, as the newly-married couple walked down the room at the end of the service, a somewhat wheezy gramophone started up the well-known strains of "Has anybody here seen Kelly?"

IN CENTRAL ALBERTA

MARLBORO, ALBERTA,
February 21st.

I RECEIVED a letter from Creighton the other day, asking me to go down and see him if possible, while he was still living in the caboose. I decided to go, and last Wednesday week left here for Edmonton, and from there, the following afternoon, went to Mirror. Mirror is on the G.T.P. line from Edmonton to Calgary, and about half-way between those two places. It is one of Creighton's headquarters, the others being Alix, Clive, and Bashaw. He has, for this country, a regular network of railways. I arrived at Mirror at 10.40 at night—distance 122 miles from Edmonton—and we took over five hours to do this, so travelling is not rapid.

I found Creighton and Cookie (the latter had been with him for some weeks) cosily established in a minute vestry which had been lately added to the Mirror Church. The church there is interesting. It was built seventeen years ago by the old-time ranchers, long before such a place as Mirror had been thought of. During the South African war two out of the five who volunteered were killed. The father of one of them has spent a lot of money on the church in memory of his son. The building is of logs, but covered with lumber and painted white, and Creighton has just designed a very pretty little steeple, which is now built and contains a bell.

The people do not appear to come to church very much, and in this respect I doubt whether an old settled district, such as this is, proves to be any the more easy to minister to than the wilder and more primitive parts where the Mission is working. Anyone coming from the Church life of the old country would most certainly consider the Church spirit out here extremely damping; but the only thing that encourages one is the hope that we are helping to build good foundations. One day there will be a more visible result of our work.

Next morning about ten, Creighton and I started in his jumper (sleigh) for Clive. He has a team of cayuses, and there was just enough snow to make sleighing possible.

The country is one of undulating hills, small valleys, and smaller lakes. The amount of water during the summer months must be very great, as in almost every valley there is a creek or a slough. Of timber there is a fair amount, though none of it is heavy, and there are acres and acres of land into which the early settlers must have been able to put their ploughs straight away. It is much like English park-land, a sort of transition stage between the bare prairies farther east and the heavier timbered country farther west. In summer it must be a beautiful part of Canada, when the trees are in full leaf and the prairie is brilliant with flowers.

There seemed to be plenty of "mixed farming" —that is, the keeping of stock besides the raising of crops. In the real prairie country, "robbing the country" is far too common. Farmers take a crop of wheat off the same land year after year, and never attempt to put back anything in the way of manure or artificial fertilisers. Before the land has given out they will probably have sold it and moved on elsewhere, and they do not think of the generation who will come after them and will be forced to pay dearly for the prodigality of the first owners. The truth is, that it is far easier for the farmer to rely on a large wheat crop than to have all the trouble of keeping stock, for which he has to put up enough hay in the summer for feed during winter. It is not at all uncommon to find the housewife on a large farm almost entirely dependent on tinned milk. Of course, there is considerable danger in staking everything on grain. If it is a bad year the farmer is done, whereas stock is always a second string to his bow. Reports tell us, however, that things are getting better, and the industry of stock-raising is reviving.

This park-like country between Edmonton and Calgary seems made for dairy-farming, and there is no doubt that the country north-west of Edmonton, where the Mission is working, will be equally good. With the advent of the railways, towns and villages will grow, and the consequent demand for dairy produce of all kinds, and for beef, will certainly be greater than the supply.

To me, of course, the main interest was the highly civilised character of the country, quite different from anything I had as yet had the opportunity of seeing in the West. It has been settled up for the past twenty years. The original settlers, at any rate round Alix, were English gentle-people of some capital. I do not think any of them have made vast sums of money by their farming, but they have just lived quietly and contentedly a country-gentleman's life. At least four families possess really nice houses. I had opportunities of seeing two of these, and they showed all the comfort and refinement of cultured English people, not unlike the houses one hears of on the big stations in Australia. For instance, the first house we called at was of the bungalow type, the ground floor one large room, with a kitchen opening out at the back and a prettily constructed staircase leading to the bedrooms above ; at one end a big open fireplace with huge logs burning on it, and in front a comfortable fender seat ; big arm-chairs and soft carpets, china and brass, and a first-class pianola; a table littered with Reviews; on the book-shelves, Walter Pater's works, Browning, William Morris, Rudyard Kipling, and Maeterlinck, and in one corner the telephone.

We arrived at Alix about lunch-time, Creighton's headquarters, and a typical little Western town of, I suppose, six hundred people. The church has been built by the well-to-do settlers around. It is well appointed, though at present its shape is curious, as it only consists of a small chancel and transept. The nave will, I suppose, be eventually added on if Alix becomes a city. Creighton's shack is quite comfortable, with writing-table, book-shelves, and piano. All the afternoon we drove through a most delightful country, frequently getting magnificent far-reaching views right away to the Red Deer Hills. Supper we had with some hospitable farmers called Shepherd, Canadians of the old-fashioned sort from Ontario, and keen Church people. After supper we drove on to Clive. At the Shepherds' none of us were certain of the right time, so Creighton telephoned to Alix and found out. The telephone is certainly most valuable, and gives outlying farms a sense of security. The difficulty is that there is only a single wire in these districts, and every time the 'phone is used all the bells in all the farmhouses ring, so you have only to take up the receiver and listen to hear the whole of the conversation between the other two parties. You can imagine that occasionally this gives rise to scandal.

The roads are well graded, and the whole country so settled up that it is all enclosed in good strong wire fences, so that if one goes across country the gates to be opened and shut are most annoying. We arrived at Clive about 9 P.M., and put up at the local hotel. Clive, though a small place, is the centre of a large farming district. It supports a doctor, on whom we called in the evening. There are numbers of doctors throughout this country—one at Alix, two at Lacombe, and one at Bashaw. How they all manage to exist I can't think. I only wish some of them would go and settle in the huge farming districts north-west of Edmonton. The Clive doctor is an Edinburgh man, and very capable. We sat talking till 10 P.M., when he was called out to a maternity case at an outlying farm.

The next morning there was a service at the church, which is a curious one. It is immense, having cost 3000 dollars, extravagantly built, and not particularly convenient now it is finished. It was built (before Creighton's time) largely to boost the town, and its huge height makes it almost impossible to heat it in the winter. There is still 1000 dollars to be paid off, which cripples the work in this part of the district.

Before the service a few children turned up for Sunday-school. There being a Methodist minister in the place, the non-Church children went to him, thus making it really much easier for the Church clergyman to go ahead and give definite Church teaching.

But north-west of Edmonton, in absolutely newly settled districts, where the Church missionary is the only official representative of religion, things are not so simple. Many of the children in our little country Sunday-schools are the children of non-Church people. Methodists, Presbyterians, Baptists, Congregationalists, Campbellites, United Brethren, &c. &c., all welcome the opportunity of having their children taught the elements of the Christian religion, but would resent anything that goes beyond that. We are often called upon to teach boys and girls who will one day grow up into strong Methodists or Presbyterians. In these settlements the actual Church people to whom we minister frequently constitute only a small percentage of the whole community. Of course our first duty is to find out and minister to the Anglican people, and this we try to do, though even the actual Church of England families are too often not over-keen to avail themselves of the ministrations of the Church.

The truth of the matter is that numbers of Church people when they come out here sink into an extraordinary state of slackness. I could give you many examples. They find it ten times more difficult to get to a service than they did when the church was at the next corner; they miss the actual building, the bells, the various parochial organisations, and all the other attractive sides of their religious life at home. Often their Churchmanship does not stand the test. They are wonderfully kind and hospitable, but when it comes to church-going they promise to come somewhat as a favour, and it is difficult when one is visiting to keep clear of the feeling that one is a kind of canvasser going round to cadge a congregation. Religion is too utterly inconvenient and opposed to the general atmosphere of the country to come easily to the Westerner.

Of course there are many shining exceptions—people who value the services, and will put themselves to considerable inconvenience to attend a celebration of the Holy Communion; but it is often noticeable that Church people tend to become imbued with a sort of undenominational fervour, and are equally ready to attend any service that may be held in the district—Anglican, Methodist, Presbyterian, Baptist, or what not. The freedom of the West infects every phase of their life, and, in showing themselves disloyal to Church principles, they imagine they are being magnanimous and charitable towards other religious bodies.

Many of the settlers with whom we have to deal out here are extremely ignorant. The Church people cannot explain why they are Church people. They come into an atmosphere where the distinctions between Protestant bodies seem of little moment, and they quickly become infected with undenominationalism. To present true Church teaching to these various sects is slow work. The broad distinction between Roman Catholicism and Protestantism is generally recognised, but to the ignorant the various Protestant bodies are much alike. Hence we sometimes find the demand for Union Churches, but we always avoid this supposed solution of the difficulty because experience proves it is unsatisfactory. If we build a church the title-deeds are in the possession of Church Trustees, and it is definitely Anglican. If some other denomination wishes to use it on some Sunday, or at some hour when we are not there, permission may be given.

Of course what I have been saying applies to newly settled rural districts only—in the cities and the older established country places every denomination has its place of worship. These small towns where Creighton is working are difficult problems for this very reason. Multiplication of churches and ministers is very depressing, and the weakness of a divided Church is particularly noticeable in a materialistic atmosphere such as the West. However, the chief duty of the Church is to witness to the Truth, and if she does that, I suppose she cannot go far wrong. At any rate all premature proposals for reunion are a tremendous mistake. The more one sees of other religious bodies, the more one realises that the Church stands for something they do not possess. In a country where all idea of discipline tends to be lightly regarded, surely the Church should give her Sacramental teaching, with its rules and requirements, absolutely fearlessly. What is needed is good sound Churchmanship and good *sound teaching*. The West is trying to assimilate thousands of home-seekers who belong to many unheard-of sects. In such an atmosphere the sane doctrines of the Church and her teaching of discipline and reverence are certainly invaluable.

Some of the other religious bodies are too apt to use their pulpits for fervid rhetoric concerning questions which border too closely on controversial politics. They do not lay much stress on discipline—reverence they have largely lost. Sometimes their services seem more to resemble an entertainment than a simple meeting together to worship God. In the West especially the Church will have to be careful not to *lay herself out* to attract. As William James says, "As soon as a Church has to be run by oysters, ice-cream, and fun, you may be sure that it is running away from Christ." Some of our people in the pioneer districts may express a desire for undenominationalism, but one often finds that such people prove to be poor Christians of any sort, and show their broad-mindedness by staying away from every kind of service.

After service we drove rapidly back to Alix, where there was a good congregation, and we had a delightful service. Afterwards we drove to Mirror, stopping at a hospitable house for tea. At Mirror, Cookie had got the church all ready for a lantern service, and soon a number of people turned up, including men from the Material gang in the yards. The slides were of the Pilgrim's Progress. We had the whole of Evensong on the screen, which is an admirable idea for a Mission Service of this kind.

We were up early on Monday morning, and had loaded the caboose and got everything ready to start by nine o'clock. Beds had to be moved in, the heater fixed up, and all manner of boxes, containing books, lanterns, crockery, and provisions. The caboose is very cosy and excellently arranged, it is eight by fifteen feet in measurement—little windows on both sides, and at one end a door—much like a gipsy wagon, except that the walls are made of canvas stretched over upright posts, then a four-inch space, and for the inside lining, birlap—a kind of canvas felt. The floor is chilly—it is only one thickness of boards, and, being lifted high on wheels, the wind and cold find it easy to penetrate. On the left is a folding

THE REV. O. CREIGHTON AND HIS CABOOSE

THE NEW NURSING HOME, ONOWAY (*north side*)

table and a low canvas chair—two camp beds, a coal-heater, on which one can cook, some shelves to hold the crockery and eatables, a few pots and pans hanging on the walls, and some sacred coloured pictures. This house on wheels is undoubtedly a good method of travelling through a country where one has no fixed head-quarters and is not well acquainted with the people. It is possible to pull it to some central place in a district, and stay there without saddling oneself on any family. There is the additional advantage of having all one's books and papers around one, and the great boon of privacy, which, however hospitable the people, is impossible when staying in a farmhouse. Creighton had so arranged one end of the caboose that it could be turned into a little chapel—a tiny altar pro-trudes about six inches from the end wall, and is covered, when not in use, by a curtain.

There was not enough snow to allow of sleighs, so the caboose travelled on strong iron wheels, behind a friendly farmer's team. Creighton, Cookie, and I travelled in the jumper. We first crossed the lower end of Buffalo Lake, so-called from its shape, which is like a buffalo's hide when stretched on the ground to dry. At the first house where we called we found there had just been an addition to the family, so did not stay. But they had a doctor and everything necessary—very different from the more distant parts north-west of Edmonton, where the woman who has a child takes her life in her hand.

From there we went on to see a young Englishman who had gone in for a special breed of horses —Suffolk punches; he had about eight stallions there—most beautiful creatures, each weighing about 1800 lbs.

The next family we found engaged in fishing in the lake. They had several holes cut through the ice, and the net stretched from hole to hole. Over the largest hole they had erected a tent and banked it up with snow; inside was a heater which kept them quite warm while they were pulling in their nets or mending them.

And so we went on all day. Creighton seemed to know everybody, but the journey gave one an idea of the immensity of these central districts of Alberta, and of the large agricultural population they support.

Towards evening we arrived at the farm where the caboose had been pulled to. On the door of the farmhouse a notice was pinned up: "Gone to town for the afternoon. Go in and make yourselves at home until we return." Truly Western hospitality! We took some of their wood, and cooked supper in the caboose, and, when the family returned, spent a delightful evening with them.

Next day we went on to Bashaw, a little town on the G.T.P., with hotel, livery barn, elevator, general stores, doctor, druggist—the whole place called into existence by a prosperous countryside and the railway. Creighton started work there some months ago, and has now got together a splendidly keen congregation.[1] A number of the people round Bashaw are English, and during the few days which I have spent in more civilised country than I have yet been in, I have seen numbers of English who have been settled here many years and are doing well.

There is a good deal of nonsense talked about the unadaptability of the English. One is always being told that the Englishman is for ever comparing his own country with the one in which he happens to be, and pointing to the superiority of England. This general criticism may have been true in the past—of some Englishmen it is perhaps true to-day; but as regards the majority, I should have said such a sweeping condemnation was somewhat unfair. From what I have seen, and from what others have told me, the average Englishman (and we have opportunity of seeing a great many absolutely new settlers) does not seem particularly aggressive with his advice, or always ready with information about "how it is done in the old country."

In some respects he Westernises himself very quickly. For instance, it does not take him long

[1] A church has since been built at Bashaw, and was dedicated in October 1913 by the Bishop of Calgary.

to adapt himself to the ideas of social equality. He often picks up Western expressions with surprising rapidity, and even cultivates the intonation of voice, so that in a few years you would put him down as a Westerner born. If he has been familiar with the land in the old country he soon "gets wise" to new conditions out here, and can often, after a short time, give the Canadian or American farmer points. What he lacks is the push and energy of those who have always been used to living in the country where all that counts is "getting there." An entirely English settlement is seldom very progressive. The presence of a few bustling Americans or Canadians creates an atmosphere of push. With them, quantity, not quality, is what matters—quantity makes more dollars than quality does. The Englishman, if he lacks push, is generally thorough at first, but soon begins to lose this characteristic and falls into Western ways, which are summed up in the expression "any old thing will do." It is regrettable, but at least a proof of his adaptability!

When I was living at Lac la Nonne, the homestead inspector for those parts, who had a large and newly settled district, told us that in his opinion nothing was more remarkable than the way in which English people, often amateur farmers and generally quite unfamiliar with the West, adapted themselves to the new conditions of life. But there is one lesson which the old country man finds hard to learn, and that is that a fellow should immediately chuck a job if it does not suit him. There is so much work out here, and so few people to do it, that no one need stay with work he does not like. Nor is change a confession of failure if the man always works hard at whatever he may be doing.

There is not the least doubt that more clergy are needed throughout this great agricultural country in a part of which Creighton is working. Almost every inch of land is taken up, and there are many places which cannot be touched through lack of men. Creighton himself is working a huge district single-handed. If he had help he could start many more centres for services, not in the little towns, which are fairly well provided for, but in the huge country districts where in some parts there is no clergyman of any kind.

In spite of the tremendous increase in the number of clergy which has taken place under the Bishop of Calgary's régime, these central parts between Calgary and Edmonton are greatly undermanned. In the *very* newest parts north and west of Edmonton, the church is keeping pace with the influx of settlers, but in Central Alberta she has not been able to do so. People, who even in their former homes were perhaps not particularly religious, naturally become callous and altogether indifferent, if left entirely without any signs of Church life.

I got back here last week, and shortly afterwards had an interesting trip to a settlement some thirty or forty miles north-east of Edson. I took the train as far as Wolf Creek, that deserted and desolated looking place which once, as the head of steel, was a town of three thousand people. From there I had to travel about twenty-five miles. I knew the country was lonely, and the pack trail (which is little more than a bridle path) somewhat difficult to find. I therefore arranged to travel with the mail carrier, who, with three or four pack ponies, fetches the mail and other necessaries from Wolf Creek once a week.

At Wolf Creek live a large family called Austin—kinder and more hospitable people you could not imagine. The father was for years Vet. to the Quorn, and one of his sons a whip. They settled on the beautiful piece of land they are now farming long before there was any railway.

Next morning, having borrowed a pony, I set off with the mail carrier. All day we made good progress through an undulating bush country, broken by several beautiful lakes. In front of us loomed the hills, from one of which, its side marked by a large patch of yellow gravel glittering in the sun, the settlement, Shining Bank, took its name. We camped twice to rest the horses and make tea. The mail carrier was most communicative and told me much about the settlement.

Towards evening signs of habitation appeared, and by 6 P.M. we were in the middle of what one day will be a fine piece of farming country—at present it is undeveloped and in the rough.

We went straight to my friend's house. He and his family inhabited a log shack on the eldest son's homestead.

"You'll stay to-night," said the goodwife hospitably, after I had put my pony in the barn.

I accepted gladly, as I knew no one in the district, but could not help wondering how we should all fit in. The shack was one-roomed, but an old and somewhat ragged curtain divided off the back part into what was evidently a bedroom, for through the curtains I could detect two large double beds. The family consisted of the father and mother, two grown-up sons, a daughter of about eighteen, and another smaller girl.

After supper I went out to visit some homesteaders near by, and about 9.30 P.M. returned. Most of the family had already turned in for the night, and as I entered my hostess called to me from behind the curtain that my bed was on the floor in the front part of the shack. All the family had apparently retired behind the curtain with the exception of the girl of eighteen and myself. She was just finishing up some work, and was evidently to sleep on the same side of the curtain as myself, on a couch which was only a few feet from my bed on the floor.

I felt the situation a little awkward, and said lengthy prayers to give her a sporting chance. Mysterious whispering and noises went on meanwhile, and when I got up the girl was in bed, her head and shoulders being hid by a table-cloth stretched across two chairs. So we live in the primitive West!

It seems almost ungracious even to describe these little incidents, when everyone is so kind and hospitable. The people at Shining Bank were all perfectly delightful, and we had a large number at service in one of the shacks on Sunday afternoon. The whole place has been worked up by Boustead, who goes up there regularly once a month, and the people evidently much appreciate his coming.

Talking of curious sleeping accommodation, some months ago now, one of our men out West was suddenly asked to go and take a funeral far away in the mountains. Two men came for him with a wagon. It was their brother who had died. The missionary of course went with them, and they drove together all day through a wild country, seeing few signs of habitation. The weather was extremely severe, the thermometer standing at 35 degrees below zero.

Long after dark they arrived at a diminutive log shack—the brothers' home. One half of the floor space was taken up by a large bed, which appeared to be the only sleeping accommodation, and on it, against the wall, lay the corpse.

That night they lit two large fires over what was to be the grave, in order to thaw the ground out.

The men had apparently felt that decency forbade the moving of the dead body. But the intense cold made the bed and the one set of blankets the only safe resting-place for the living, so all had to get into the one bed for the night. As the missionary was the only one to say his prayers, he allowed the others to get into bed before him, and so avoided sleeping next to the corpse.

NEEDS AND EXPERIMENTS

THREE PRESSING NEEDS OF THE CHURCH IN THE NEW DIOCESE OF EDMONTON

(1) *An Anglican College at the University.*

CROWNING the steep, wooded banks of the Saskatchewan River, and occupying one of the most prominent positions in the whole of Edmonton, capital city of the province, stand the beginnings of a great University. Born only a few years ago, the University of Alberta has already become one of the great educational centres of the West. It can only be a question of time before it has attained a position of national importance.

Universities in a new country must assuredly justify their *raison d'être* if they are to live and flourish. The wonderful progress of the University of Alberta, from the very day on which it first opened its lecture-rooms to students, proves to what an extent it has been able both to create and satisfy a demand for higher education.

And indeed, under the brilliant guidance of its President, Dr. H. M. Tory, the University touches the life of the community at many points. In the first place, it is training men and women who will be called upon to occupy positions of trust and responsibility in every department of life throughout the West. As teachers, doctors, clergy, lawyers, farmers, engineers, politicians, and as leaders of thought and action in many other spheres, it is clear that the alumni of this University will not only be found in every avenue leading into public life, but will also be well qualified to shape the destinies of the next generation.

Further, many of the learned associations of Alberta are affiliated with the University—*e.g.* the College of Physicians and Surgeons of Alberta, the Alberta Architects' Association, the Alberta Land Surveyors, and the Law Society of Alberta. The examinations of these various associations have been put in the hands of the University Senate, on which in return each Society is represented.

Then, again, a thorough system of extension work is being carried on by a department created for the purpose. Courses of lectures are given in the larger towns throughout the province, debating societies are encouraged, definite courses of study suggested for individuals, and in every way attempts are being made to bring the University into the closest possible touch with the lives of the people.

The University grants a free site of about seven

acres of land to any of the affiliating bodies who wish to erect buildings. So far, the Methodists and Presbyterians are the only religious bodies who are providing for their own men. The University has two large Halls where a number of the students reside, but each denomination is encouraged to take advantage of the free site offered and establish its own college.

Whether good or bad, the system of denominational colleges in affiliation with the University is a common feature of academic life in Canada; and at a great educational institution, such as the University of Alberta, it is of the very first importance that the Anglican Church should be represented in a manner worthy of her distinguished past in Eastern Canada and of her still greater future in the New West.

We need, not a theological hostel, but a college of the widest character, neither more nor less denominational than a college at Oxford or Cambridge. Any student, no matter what future career he was preparing himself for, would be welcomed; but residence would imply a willingness to conform to the discipline of the college. The men residing in such a college would probably be of three kinds—(1) the large majority would be reading Arts, Law, Medicine, and other schools, fitting them for many and various professions. (2) There would be some who had taken their B.A. at the University and were staying on to go through a course of theology in the college. (3) There would probably be a certain number of graduates of other universities who had come to the college merely to study theology.

A college, capable of providing comfortable residential accommodation for its students, worthy both in architecture and equipment of the position it would occupy in a great University, and possessing in its chapel the symbols of its own highest ideals, would not only be rooted in the great traditions of the Anglican Church in the past, but would also help to realise the pressing needs of to-day.

(2) *A School.*

The whole educational system of Alberta leads up to the University. So also there should be a first-class private school leading up to and in close connection with the Anglican College. Every year the number of parents who are in a position to pay higher fees for the education of their children increases, and consequently there is a growing need for private schools, such as exist in Eastern Canada, where there is much to remind one of all that is best in the life of an old English public school. The relationship of Trinity College School, Port Hope, to Trinity College at the University of Toronto, is a case in point.

With the exception of that given in Roman Catholic separate schools, there is no religious teaching of any kind in the public (*i.e.* Board) schools of Alberta.[1] It is to be greatly hoped that before long all other denominations will avail themselves of their rights, and insist on religion forming some part of the curriculum. Steps are being taken to present a united front on this matter.

In a country progressing so rapidly as the West, the success which would attend a good private school, if such were started near Edmonton, is certain, and the Church must surely see to it that, at any rate in this type of school, first-class secular education should not be divorced from sound religious teaching.

For Southern Alberta, the Bishop Pinkham College supplies the need. Its history shows in the most emphatic way how real is the demand for such schools. Bishop Pinkham College was opened in 1911, and during the first year the enrolment of pupils was 41. The following season, 1912–1913, though the dormitory accommodation was almost doubled, every bed was occupied. Applications had to be refused. The buildings having once been erected, the school is self-supporting. A school on the lines of Bishop Pinkham's is an urgent need for the

[1] Except in country schools under certain conditions before mentioned, p. 97.

new diocese of Edmonton. Distances are so great that it would draw on parts of the province far removed from Southern Alberta. In combination with a college at the University, to which a large number of the boys would naturally pass on, the influence on the community of such a school might be great, not only by the clear enunciation of religious principles, but also by the atmosphere of responsibility and service which are the fruit of religious convictions.

Further, the establishment of a school and college would help towards the solution of one of the greatest problems with which the Canadian Church in general, and especially that branch of it in the West, is faced. Of the Western clergy, comparatively few are Canadian trained, still fewer Canadian born. Owing to the overwhelming influx of people, it is not to be wondered at that the Canadian Church has been forced to draw upon England for her clergy. But if she is to be truly a Canadian Church for the Canadian people, this method of recruiting her ranks must cease. Her clergy must be Canadians, trained in Canadian schools and Canadian universities, and familiar from the first with Canadian habits of life. The great work achieved in this respect by the famous St. John's School and Theological College at Winnipeg, revived in 1866 by Archbishop Machray, is an eloquent proof of what might be done by similar institutions in the farther North-West, no longer the exclusive property of the fur-trader, but the home of a young and progressive people.

(3) *Nursing Home and Medical Help for the Country Districts.*[1]

The pioneer expects hardship, and glories in it. But there is one form of hardship which he dreads, the difficulty, and sometimes the impossibility, of obtaining the help of medical or nursing skill in case of accident and sickness. Where he has wife and children with him, this hardship fills his mind with haunting care. Over many a vast area of the West the settler of to-day is scarcely more fortunate in this regard than the pioneer of earlier days. Doctors are provided by the railways for the men engaged on construction work ; doctors settle in the little towns that spring up along the railways, but very rarely, if ever, is a nurse or a doctor to be found in the country districts. In the area entrusted by the Bishop of Calgary to the Edmonton Mission, reaching roughly 200 miles from east to west and 70 miles from north to south, there is not a single authorised medical practitioner, except along the two railways, the one running on the south and

[1] The following paragraphs are adapted, by permission, from an article written by the Rev. W. G. Boyd which appeared in *Church Life* in August 1913.

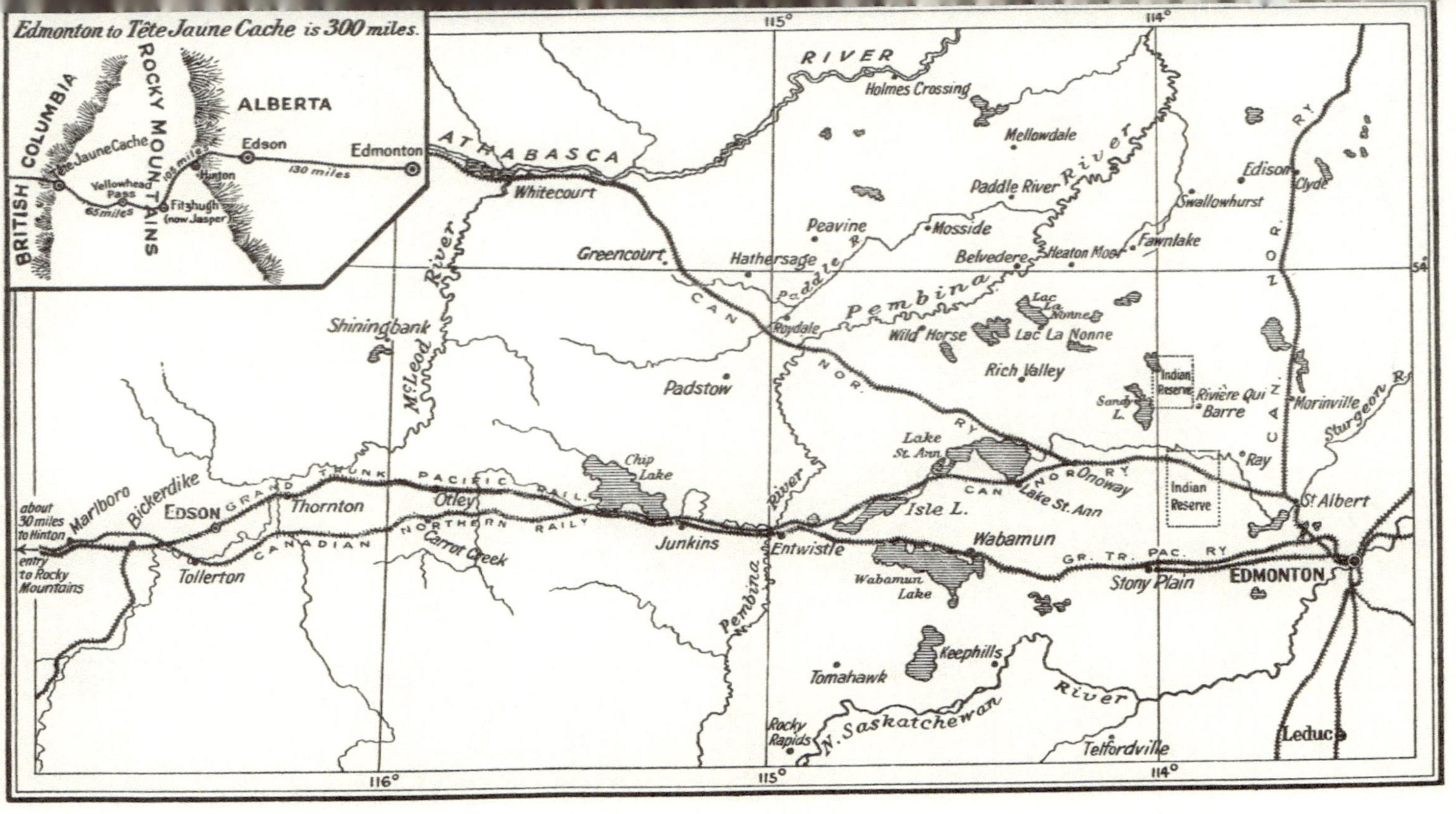

MAP SHOWING THE DISTRICT OF THE EDMONTON MISSION
(Only the more important settlements are given)
(Inset, the Yellowhead Pass over the Rockies)

the other on the east side of this parallelogram. Anyone who knows anything of the life of the homesteading population knows how much unnecessary suffering, harassing anxiety, and often loss of life is involved in this state of things.

A few weeks ago a woman was taken ill before confinement. There was no help near, and the husband could not leave her. At last he had to start with her in his wagon to the nearest town, 70 miles away. She was ill on the way, and he could find no place to take her to but an empty shack. Here the poor fellow had to sit helpless, and see his wife die.

Two nurses were recently paying a visit to friends some distance north-west of Edmonton; they were out for a holiday, but were scarcely ever without a call for their nursing skill. A boy got a finger caught in a circular saw, and came 5 miles every other day to have it treated. A delicate woman was awaiting her confinement with the nearest doctor 30 miles off. Whilst her husband went for him no one was with her but a half-breed woman who could not speak English. This had been her experience at the birth of each of three children previously born.

The generosity of a lady in England, who has undertaken to provide the stipends of two nurses for at least a year, has made it possible for an experiment to be made in connection with the Edmonton Mission, and on 7th August 1913,

St. Barnabas' Nursing Home, which is to be the headquarters for the work, was opened at Onoway, 40 miles west of Edmonton, by Miss Pinkham, the daughter of the Bishop of Calgary. In a pretty situation on the side of a hill, a frame building on a concrete basement has been put up. The entrance is at the back on the north into a central hall, out of which open three wards (for four patients), a little operating theatre, and a lavatory. Along the front, on the south side of the house, is a verandah on to which through wide doors patients' beds can be wheeled. Downstairs in the basement, which is on the south side above the level of the ground and well lighted, are the nurses' dining-room, the kitchen, and laundry, besides furnace-room and cold storage. Upstairs are the nurses' bedrooms, bathroom, linen cupboard, and a beautiful little chapel.

Two English nurses, excellently qualified for the life, have given themselves to the work for a comparatively small stipend, and a doctor, who has had experience in England and abroad, has settled in Onoway, and will work in connection with the Mission. The experiment has been made, but it is impossible to say if the difficulties of the situation can be altogether overcome. How far afield will the benefit of the home be felt? The trails being what they are, people 50 miles away will still have to face a terrible journey before they can get into the home. Will it be possible to carry out anything in the nature of district work? The population is very sparse; it may take a nurse all day to visit a single patient 15 miles away, and she may have no other to visit in the same direction. These are questions which experience alone can answer.

Then there is the question of finance. How far can such a Nursing Home be expected to be self-supporting? Clearly, not altogether or at first. Even in cities, hospitals are not as a rule self-supporting, and the homesteading population is poor. Every cent they can put into their homestead in the way of buildings, stock, or implements hastens the day when they will begin to make money. It is certain, then, that they cannot afford to pay high fees. It is because the cost of getting a doctor or nurse from town is prohibitive, that so many have to face sickness without any efficient help at all. The aim of the Mission is to provide the very best skill and care at a price which the farmer can pay. The people for the most part will gratefully contribute up to the very limit of their power, and sometimes it may be possible to accept payment in kind or in labour upon the Mission farm. When the work is established, and can be shown to be effective, the Provincial Government will be asked to help.

The building of the little hospital has been expensive. Water had to be laid on from a spring 300 yards away, and a heating system installed. The freighting of material to the site has proved costly. The total sum for building and furnishing is likely to be 10,000 dollars; of this sum 6000 dollars have been contributed.

(4) *The Archbishops' Western Canada Fund. Its Temporary Character.*

After careful consultation with the authorities of the Church in Canada, the Archbishops' Western Canada Fund was launched in the spring of 1910 by a joint appeal from the Archbishops of Canterbury and York. It was decided to establish three separate Missions—one with its headquarters at Edmonton, under the Rev. W. G. Boyd; a second in Southern Alberta, to work in the neighbourhood of Lethbridge and Cardston, under the Rev. W. H. Mowatt; a third with its centre at Regina, capital of the province of Saskatchewan, under the Rev. D. Ellison.

In Saskatchewan rapid railway construction had brought into existence a number of small towns, and it was important that the Church should minister both to these and to the agricultural country in their vicinity. In Southern Alberta the problem was urgent, largely owing to the fact that Cardston had been made the centre for

Canadian Mormonism. In the country north-west of Edmonton the land had either been occupied for a short time or was rapidly being taken up, thus giving opportunity for the Church to "start in" with the settler.

The appeal met with considerable support,[1] and in May 1910, the Rev. W. G. Boyd, with six men, arrived at Edmonton. The same year work was started in Southern Alberta and Saskatchewan.

Since that time the three Missions have steadily grown, and recently the Fund has made itself responsible for two extensive districts, one in the Saskatchewan and the other in the Athabasca Diocese. The members of the three original Missions combined number between sixty and seventy men, about half of whom are clergy and half laymen.

From the first it was seen that layworkers should be able to do valuable work for the Church in the West. As regards the Edmonton Mission, it was decided to appeal (i.) to men who had not had an University education in England, but who were willing, after having been trained for the ministry and ordained in Canada, to give some years of work to the Dominion; and (ii.) to graduates of "old country" universities who,

[1] From Easter 1910 to Easter 1913 about £78,000 was received Out of this sum considerable grants have been made each year to the other societies already working in Canada.

whether or not they had made up their minds with regard to ordination at some future time, were willing to give at least two years of work to the Mission. The first part of the scheme did not meet with great success, chiefly because the Church possessed, and still possesses, no college in connection with the University of Alberta. Under the second part of the scheme, I was the first to go out to Edmonton in April 1911, and since that time five or six other graduates of Oxford or Cambridge have joined Mr. Boyd.

At the present time all three branches of the Archbishops' Mission in the West have a certain number of graduate laymen on their staff, and, if the men are forthcoming, there seems to be no reason why this side of the work should not be further developed. Speaking from my own experience, I feel tolerably certain that no one who felt able to cast in his lot with the Mission, for a couple of years after taking his degree, would have reason to regret his decision. There is a wonderful fascination in playing a rôle, however humble, in the building up of what will be one of the most influential nations in world politics. If it happens that these lines are read by someone who, nearing the end of his 'Varsity career, is still uncertain about his next step, let him ask himself, not if there is any reason why he should, but if there is any reason why he should not undertake this work for his Church.

There is one department of the Edmonton Mission which has been hardly so much as mentioned in the foregoing pages. I refer to the ladies' work, the importance of which it would be difficult to exaggerate. Sister Mary and Miss Warden went out to Edmonton in the spring of 1911, and shortly afterwards a house was built for them on the Mission property. Sister Mary had unfortunately to return to England in 1913, but Miss Warden still remains in charge of this branch of the work, and the extraordinary variety of occupations which falls to her lot is in itself ample proof of the value of her presence. Her knowledge of nursing enabled Miss Warden to take a prominent part in the organisation of the little country hospital at Onoway, and there are few women's organisations in Alberta working for the good of the community with which she is not connected.

In 1910, the Archbishops appealed for men and money. Three years later they reiterated the appeal, laying special stress on the temporary character of the whole scheme. "We are encouraged to believe," they write in Easter 1913, "that we were right in our original estimate that the critical period would be the next ten years. Three of these have already passed.[1] We desire to emphasize this temporary character of our appeal,

[1] Practically four years have now (Feb. 1914) passed since the three Missions were established.

and the consequent necessity of its receiving adequate response at a juncture of supreme importance."

And, indeed, it is clear that a few years will see the Church in Canada occupying a far stronger position than is hers perhaps to-day. The amazing rush to both Eastern and Western Canada cannot continue at its present rate. With the decrease of immigration, the unparalleled strain of these wonderful years will, to a large extent, be removed, and the Church will at any rate be able to face the enormous task of developing and strengthening the work she has already begun without the heartrending knowledge that there are still huge stretches of country where she is entirely unrepresented. In time to come, the Church in the West will be able to look back and see that she was helped by the Archbishops' Mission to traverse a period in her history, which posterity will judge to have been unprecedented in the life of this or any nation.

APPENDIX

Summary for Canada of all Religions in 1911 Compared with 1901

Religions.	1911.	1901.
Adventists	10,406	8,058
Agnostics	3,110	3,613
Anglicans	1,043,017	681,494
Apostles	28	-
Armenians	15	-
Baptists	382,666	318,005
Believers	582	495
Bible Christians	101	-
Bible Students	518	-
Brethren	9,278	8,014
Buddhists	10,012	10,407
Calvinists	151	43
Carmelites	101	27
Catholic Apostolic	830	400
Christadelphians	1,326	1,030
Christians	16,773	6,900
Christian Alliance	113	-
Christian Brethren	350	266
Christian Catholics	22	124
Christian Church	135	-
Christian Science	5,073	2,619
Christian Workers	491	584
Church of Christ	3,225	2,264
Church of God	1,094	351
Church Workers	436	-
Confucians	14,562	5,115
Congregationalists	34,054	28,293
Covenanters	88	17
Daniel's Band	64	31
Deists	34	78
Disciples	11,329	14,900
Dissenters	55	-
Doukhobors	10,493	8,775
Evangelicals	10,595	10,193
Exclusive Brethren	14	-
Farrington Independents	156	16
Free Church	278	30
Friends	4,027	4,100

The Land of Open Doors

Religions.	1911.	1901.
Gospel People	512	135
Greek Church	88,507	15,630
Holy Rollers	20	–
Hornerites	3,856	2,775
Independents	430	–
Jews	74,564	16,401
Lutherans	229,864	92,524
Marshallites	42	–
Mennonites	44,611	31,797
Methodists	1,079,892	916,886
Millennial Dawnites	407	99
Mission	863	–
Mohammedans	797	47
Mormons	15,971	6,891
New Church	1,019	881
Nonconformists	540	–
Non-Sectarians	1,118	215
No religion	26,027	4,810
Pagans	11,840	15,107
Pentecostal Movement	513	–
Plymouth Brethren	3,088	2,774
Presbyterians	1,115,324	842,442
Protestants	30,265	11,612
Reformed Church	922	20
Roman Catholics	2,833,041	2,229,600
Saints	297	–
Saints of God	39	10
Salvation Army	18,834	10,308
Shintos	1,289	–
Sikhs and Hindus	1,758	–
Socialists	206	–
Spiritualists	674	616
Theosophists	177	107
Undenominationalists	290	–
Unionists	633	29
Unitarians	3,224	1,934
United Brethren	4,333	4,701
United Free	19	–
Universalists	1,995	2,589
Welsh Church	55	–
Zionites (Dowieites)	55	42
Various Sects	640	869
Unspecified	32,490	43,222

LONDON: WELLS GARDNER, DARTON AND CO., LTD.

THE SOCIAL HISTORY OF CANADA

General Editor: Michael Bliss

1 **The Wretched of Canada: Letters to R.B. Bennett 1930-1935**
Edited and introduced by L.M. Grayson and Michael Bliss

2 **Canada and the Canadian Question**
Goldwin Smith
Introduction, Carl Berger

3 **My Neighbor**
J.S. Woodsworth
Introduction, Richard Allen

4 **The Bunkhouse Man**
E.W. Bradwin
Introduction, Jean Burnet

5 **In Times Like These**
Nellie McClung
Introduction, Veronica Strong-Boag

6 **The City below the Hill**
A.B. Ames
Introduction, Paul Rutherford

7 **Strangers within Our Gates**
J.S. Woodsworth
Introduction, Marilyn Barber

8 **The Rapids**
Alan Sullivan
Introduction, Michael Bliss

9 **Philosophy of Railroads and Other Essays**
T.C. Keefer
Introduction, H.V. Nelles

10 **The Americanization of Canada 1907**
Samuel E. Moffett
Introduction, Allan Smith

11 **Rural Life in Canada: Its Trend and Tasks**
John MacDougall
Introduction, R. Craig Brown

12 **The New Christianity**
Salem Bland
Introduction, Richard Allen

13 **Canadian Investigates Industrialism: The Royal Commission on the Relations of Labor and Capital**
Edited and introduced by Greg Kealey

14 **Industry and Humanity**
William Lyon Mackenzie King
Introduction, David Jay Bercuson

15 **The Social Criticism of Stephen Leacock: The Unsolved Riddle of Social Justice and Other Essays**
Stephen Leacock
Edited and introduced by Alan Bowker

16 **A Dutch Homesteader on the Prairies: The Letters of Willem De Gelder**
Willem De Gelder
Translated and introduced by H. Ganzevoort

17 **The Tragedy of Quebec: The Expulsion of its Protestant Farmers**
Robert Sellar
Introduction, Robert Hill

18 **The Woman Suffrage Movement in Canada**
Catherine L. Cleverdon
Introduction, Ramsay Cook

19 **The Queen v Louis Riel**
Introduction, Desmond Morton

20 **The Writing on the Wall**
Hilda Glynn-Ward
Introduction, Patricia E. Roy

21 **By Great Waters: A Newfoundland and Labrador Anthology**
Edited and introduced by Peter Neary and Patrick O'Flaherty

22 **Saving the Canadian City. The First Phase 1880-1920: An Anthology of Articles on Urban Reform**
Edited and introduced by Paul Rutherford

23 **The Magpie**
Douglas Durkin
Introduction, Peter E. Rider

24 **Report on Social Security for Canada**
Leonard Marsh
New introduction by the author

25 **A History of Farmers' Movements in Canada**
Louis Aubrey Wood
Foster J.K. Griezic

26 **Social Planning for Canada**
League for Social Reconstruction
Introduction, F.R. Scott, Leonard Marsh, Graham Spry, J. King Gordon, E.A. Forsey, and J.F. Parkinson

27 **For My Country (Pour la patrie)**
Jules-Paul Tardivel
Translation, Sheila Fischman
Introduction, A.I. Silver

28 **The Politics of Labor**
T. Phillips Thompson
Introduction, Jay Atherton

29 **The Land of Open Doors Being Letters from Western Canada 1911-13**
J. Burgon Bickersteth
New introduction by the author

Available in cloth and paper editions

www.ingramcontent.com/pod-product-compliance
Lightning Source LLC
Chambersburg PA
CBHW050616110726
47899CB00001B/136

* 9 7 8 0 8 0 2 0 6 2 6 6 6 *